LIVING SACRIFICES

AND

MESSAGE OF CROSS

LESLIE M. JOHN

LIVING SACIFICES

AND

MESSAGE OF CROSS

LESLIE M. JOHN

It is imperative that a Christian should have a good knowledge about the sacrifices and oblations offered in the Old Testament because they form the foundational truth to substantiate the crucifixion and resurrection of Lord Jesus Christ.

DESCRIPTON:

This book brings out the Truth of the knowledge that Lord Jesus Christ is the only high Priest and mediator between God and man, and there is no salvation except in Him and by Him. It also lays out a clear picture of sacrifices and oblations offered in the Old Testament period and as to how they were foreshadows of the substance that was revealed in the New Testament and It presents as to how they were related to the spiritual sacrifices and oblations offered in the New Testament.

ABOUT THE AUTHOR:

The author, who accepted Lord Jesus Christ as his personal Savior when he was a boy of 13, was raised in a Christian family in India and had education in Christian Institutions.

This then was the message that he heard of the Son of God, Lord Jesus Christ. This then is the message that he declares that God is light and in Him there is no darkness at all. Jesus Christ is the Son of God sent from above to save sinners.

Jesus died on the cross bearing our sins upon Himself. He was buried and God raised Him on the third day. Jesus, after having appeared to many for 40 days ascended to heaven. He will come again. Whosoever confesses his/her sins to Him and believe in heart that God raised Him from the dead will not perish but will have everlasting life.

"Jesus saith unto him, I am the way, the truth, and the life: no man cometh unto the Father, but by me" (John 14:6).

SCRIPTURES

Scriptures quoted in this book are from KJV from open domain, and from NIV, ESV, and NLT not greater than the number permitted.

ISBN 13: 978-0-9985181-2-1

ISBN 10: 09985181-2-3

TABLE OF CONTENTS

CHAPTER 1

CHRIST ENTERED INTO HEAVEN

"For Christ is not entered into the holy places made with hands, which are the figures of the true; but into heaven itself, now to appear in the presence of God for us: Nor yet that he should offer himself often, as the high priest entereth into the holy place every year with blood of others" (Hebrews 9:24-25)

It is beyond imagination for a believer in Christ the privilege he/she has in approaching God so freely through Lord Jesus Christ, the one only mediator, who is the high priest, of the order of Melchisedec. A child of God would humble before the Lord and acknowledge His sacrifice of His own body and blood shed on the Cross.

While the priests in the Old Testament period offered sacrifices of animals that reminded them of their sins incessantly, we in the New Testament period, are so blessed that we do not need to offer animal sacrifices, inasmuch as Lord Jesus Christ entered into heaven and is seated on the right hand of the Majesty after purging our sins.

We recollect Lord Jesus Christ's crucifixion, burial and His resurrection, and thank Him for His sacrifice rather than recollecting our past sins. God promised us that He will not remember our sins.

When the LORD looks at us through the blood shed on behalf of us for the remission of our sins, we appear to Him as clear and clean as a crystal would look like.

An atheist or one who is pride seldom thanks God for what he is. He rather considers his elevated current position in society that he rightly deserves is because of his hard work. He would hardly spare time to thank God. He boasts on his achievements, and thinks that he deserves the blessings. He would give credit to his own works, virtue and efforts rather than recognizing the grace of God.

Most Christians do not ponder over the hardship the Old Testament believers faced in approaching God. When Moses was called to go up the Mount Sinai to speak to God, not a single man was allowed to go near the mountain. If they did, they would surely realize that we, in the New Testament period are far more blessed than those in the Old Testament period.

We are indeed so comfortable in approaching the Father because of the freedom that we received by the sacrifice of Lord Jesus Christ, of His own body and blood on behalf of us.

The study of high priest, priests and their service in the Tabernacle, and the offerings and sacrifices that they had offer year after year on behalf of children of Israel, helps us to appreciate the freedom we enjoy in Christ.

The LORD said to Moses to tell Aaron, after the death of Nadab and Abib, sons of Aaron not to go into the most holy place in the Tabernacle as and when he wishes to do, but one in a year complying with all the requirements God laid down in Leviticus 16:1-34.

There was a very meticulous method specified by God. The LORD gave specific instructions to Aaron by Moses that if he violated any minute detail of the specific instructions Aaron would die instantly.

Except for Aaron, none else was permitted to be in the Tabernacle on the "Day of Atonement", which is tenth day of the seventh month of the year, of which the first month was "Abib" renamed later as "Nissan".

"And it shall be a statute to you forever that in the seventh month, on the tenth day of the month, you shall afflict yourselves2 and shall do no work, either the native or the stranger who sojourns among you. 30 For on this day shall atonement be made for you to cleanse you. You shall be clean before the Lord from all your sins" (Lev. 16:29, 30)

The Types and shadows are no more there after Lord Jesus Christ has fulfilled the law. In the sacrifices that were offered by the children of Israel in the Old Testament period there was a reminder of sins every year, because it was impossible for the blood of bulls and goats to fully expiate sins of the one on whose behalf the sacrifice was offered.

Eventually in accordance with the prophecies mentioned in the books of law, prophets, and Psalms, Lord Jesus came into this world in the form of a servant in the likeness of man to fulfill the desire of the Father in heaven (cf. Hebrews 10:3-7).

In the New Testament period we, the children of God, are instructed to offer living sacrifices. A believer in Christ does not need to offer animal sacrifices or human sacrifices. It is, therefore, imperative that every child of God should offer spiritual sacrifices.

We are living stones of the spiritual house being built by God We are holy priesthood, to offer up spiritual sacrifices acceptable to God, by His one only Son, Lord Jesus Christ.

"As you come to him, a living stone rejected by men but in the sight of God chosen and precious, you yourselves like living stones are being built up as pa spiritual house, to be a holy priesthood, to offer spiritual sacrifices acceptable to God through Jesus Christ" 1 Peter 2:4-5)

"But you are a chosen race, a royal priesthood, a holy nation, da people for his own possession, that you may proclaim the Excellencies of him who called you out of darkness into his marvelous light" (1 Peter 2:9)

CHAPTER 2

MELCHISEDEC

Melchisedec was a type of Christ in person and dignity.

The writer of Hebrews compares Melchisedec with Lord Jesus Christ and finds that Melchisedec was a type of Christ in dignity and in person. He was king of Salem, the priest of Almighty God, who met Abraham when the latter was returning after slaughtering the kings for kidnapping his brother's son Lot and his possessions including women and people.

Melchisedec was not a Levite because there were no Levites at his time. It may recalled that the Abraham's son was Isaac, and Isaac's son was Jacob, who was renamed by God as "Israel". Jacob had twelve sons, and one of the twelve tribes from these twelve sons, was the tribe of Levi, who were chosen as priests of God, and they are called Aaronic order of priests. Aaron was the first high priest appointed by God through His servant Moses. Therefore, it is obvious that Melchisedec was fully outsider from the clan of Israel. In a very similar manner Lord Jesus Christ, who was a descendant of Abraham, Isaac, and Jacob, and came from the lineage of King David, and yet He was not from the lineage of Levites. Thus he was not from the Aaronic priesthood, but of Judah.

CHAPTER 3

OF THE ORDER OF MELCHISEDEC

This prophecy is corroborated by the writing in Hebrews 5:5-6 where it says that Christ did not glorify Himself to be made as high priest, but the Father declared Him as the high priest after the order of Melchisedec.

"So also Christ glorified not himself to be made a high priest; but he that said unto him, Thou art my Son, today have I begotten thee. As he saith also in another place, Thou art a priest forever after the order of Melchisedec" (Hebrews 5:5-6).

The high priesthood of Lord Jesus Christ is greater than the Aaronic priesthood. The narration as to how Lord Jesus Christ is superior to Aaronic priesthood is based on scriptures in Genesis 14:18-20, and Hebrews 7:1-28.

Abram and Lot separated themselves in order to avoid confrontation of their herdsmen with one another. Lot lifted up his eyes and saw the plain of Jordan was pleasant and fertile (before Jehovah destroyed Sodom and Gomorrah), and therefore, he chose the said land for his stay, while Abram lived in the land of Canaan (cf. Genesis 13:10-12)

The five-king confederation, while attacking four king confederation for their rebellion, as described in Genesis 14:1-12, took away Lot and all his possessions including women and people. When Abram heard of the loot by the five kings, he decided to fight them and get back Lot and all his property as also women and people.

Abram went forth pursuing the five-king confederation as far as Dan. He divided his 318 trained servants of his household into two at night and pursued them up to Hobah, which is north of Damascus and defeated them. He recovered all the belongings of Lot and Lot himself, and women and the people and returned to his place. King of Sodom went and met Abram and requested Abram to keep for himself the entire goods that he won, but return only the people. However, Abram refused to keep any extra possessions than that belonged to Lot. He returned people and the goods to king of Sodom and gave away Lot's possessions to Lot.

In the meanwhile, Melchizedek, who was the priest of the Almighty God, and a king of Salem, brought to Abram bread and wine, and blessed Abram and said "Blessed be Abram of the most high God, possessor of heaven and earth: And blessed be the most high God, which hath delivered thine enemies into thy hand. And he gave him tithes of all. (Genesis 14:18-20).

Interesting to observe that Lord Jesus Christ in the New Testament period "...took bread, and blessed it, and broke it and gave it to the disciples and said, 'Take, eat; this is my body. And he took the cup, and gave thanks, and gave it to them, saying, drink you all of it; for this is my blood of the New Testament, which is shed for many for the remission of sins" (Matthew 26:26-28)

The writer of Hebrews quotes in Hebrews 7:1-28, this incident of Melchizedek the priest of Almighty God blessing Abram and receiving Tithe from Abram and analyzes to bring forth a great truth that Lord Jesus Christ is the high priest of the order of Melchizedek. The writer says this Melchisedec, who was King of Salem is by interpretation the king of righteousness, and King of Salem by interpretation is the King of peace. There is neither any history of his antecedents nor of his descendants. He has neither beginning of days, nor the end of his life, but He resembled Lord Jesus Christ, continues to be the priest forever. Lord Jesus Christ said of Himself in Revelation 1:11 that He is Alpha and Omega, the first and the last.

CHAPTER 4

SUPERIORITY OF LORD JESUS CHRIST

"But unto the Son he saith, Thy throne, O God, is for ever and ever: a scepter of righteousness is the scepter of thy kingdom" (Hebrews 1:8; cf. Psalm 45:6-7)

Two prophecies come into our minds where the superiority in position of Lord Jesus Christ over angels and Aaronic priesthood are shown.

First prophecy is from Psalm 2:7 where Jehovah declares that Lord Jesus Christ is His Son, and that the LORD has begotten Him. It is evident that Jehovah never called angels as begotten ones.

"I will declare the decree: the LORD hath said unto me, Thou art my Son; this day have I begotten thee". (Psalms 2:7)

The writer of Hebrews questions if God had called, at any time, angels as His begotten ones; the answer is clear. The LORD God Jehovah never called any angel as His angel as His begotten one, while at the same He called Lord Jesus Christ as His begotten one.

"For unto which of the angels said he at any time, Thou art my Son, this day have I begotten thee? And again, I will be to him a Father, and he shall be to me a Son?" (Hebrews 1:5)

Begotten here does not mean Jesus was His physical son born to Him, but it means The LORD manifested Lord Jesus as the

Messiah. God is a Spirit, and He has no offspring by any means, excepting for declaring Lord Jesus Christ as His Son. It is very important to note that while declaring so, Jehovah calls Him as God; thus showing that Lord Jesus Christ is equal with Himself.

The Son also says that He and His Father are one.

"I and my Father are one" (John 10:30)

Apostle Paul writes in Philippians 2:6-7 that Jesus did not consider to be equal with God in glory while descending on to this earth in the form of a servant and in the likeness of man, inasmuch as His whole purpose was to become a substitute sacrifice for the sins of the mankind that whosoever believes in Him shall not perish but have everlasting life.

Second prophecy is from Psalm 110:4 where Lord Jesus Christ's high priesthood is prophesied.

"The LORD hath sworn, and will not repent, Thou art a priest forever after the order of Melchizedek" (Psalms 110:4)

CHAPTER 5

WHY COMPARE CHRIST WITH MELCHISEDEC?

Fundamentally, it was because Aaronic priesthood, in which Jews strongly held their beliefs, was deficient. Jewish Christians in the centuries that followed immediately of Lord Jesus Christ's crucifixion, burial, resurrection and ascension were reluctant to give up their traditional rituals of animal sacrifices for the remission of their sins.

In fact, animal sacrifice never removed sins of any one fully but only covered temporarily until the perfect sacrifice was offered by Lord Jesus Christ of His own body and precious blood for the remission of sins of mankind. Thus a permanent provision is made for forgiveness of sins of mankind provided sinner accepts Lord Jesus Christ as his/her savior and believes that the Lord died for his sins, and was buried and on the third day rose from the dead and later ascended into heaven.

After purging sins of mankind the Lord ascended into heaven and seated on the right hand of the Majesty and pleading on our behalf. Thus fulfilling literally the requirement of Old Testament high priest entering into Most Holy place in the Tabernacle once a year with the blood of animals sacrificed and sprinkling on the Mercy Seat. Lord Jesus Christ is continually pleading on behalf of us in the heavenly sanctuary, with the Father, of our shortcomings, while the adversary (Satan) is continuously accusing believers in Christ before the Jehovah, the Father.

Jehovah, the Almighty God sees the blood of Jesus Christ shed for the sins of mankind and the cleansing of the sins done by the Lord's blood, and sees no sin in the person, who was a sinner but believed in Lord Jesus Christ as Savior.

Early Jewish Christians could not fully fathom the way their sins are purged and forgiven by Lord Jesus Christ. This dilemma made some of them to backslide or refuse to believe in the efficacy of the blood of Lord Jesus Christ that cleanses the sin of the sinner. Therefore, a reasonable explanation was given to them by the writer of Hebrews clearly showing the superiority of Lord Jesus Christ over everyone, and everything in the world.

This preaching is indeed foolishness to those who do not understand the reason why Jesus died for our sins and was buried and rose from the dead on the third day and later ascended into heaven. However, for those who are saved it is the power of God. Apostle Paul writes…

"For the preaching of the cross is to them that perish foolishness; but unto us which are saved it is the power of God". *(1 Corinthians 1:18)*

Lord Jesus Christ said very emphatically that

"Jesus answered and said unto him, Verily, verily, I say unto thee, except a man be born again, he cannot see the kingdom of God". *(John 3:3)*

Nicodemus did not understand the words of Lord Jesus. He inquired from the Lord as to how a man can be born again when he is old. His dilemma increased and asked Jesus if a man should enter his mother's womb once again to be born again. The Lord replied to him "that which is born of flesh is flesh: and that is born of the Spirit is spirit".

It is the spiritual birth that matters. Everyone born into this world dies and dust that he is, returns to dust. However, the inner man (the Soul and spirit) of every individual will either live eternally with God, if the individual is saved, or else his soul and spirit will be cast into the "lake of fire", where gnashing of teeth never stops nor does thirst quench (cf. John 3:3-7; Rev 19:20; 20:10,14-15).

The only way suggested in the Bible for man to receive everlasting life is by accepting Lord Jesus Christ as personal Savior, and there is absolutely no other way.

"That if thou shalt confess with thy mouth the Lord Jesus, and shalt believe in thine heart that God hath raised him from the dead, thou shalt be saved. For with the heart man believeth unto righteousness; and with the mouth confession is made unto salvation" (Romans 10:9-10)

"Neither is there salvation in any other: for there is none other name under heaven given among men, whereby we must be saved" (Acts 4:12).

CHAPTER 6

SIGNIFICANCE OF PAYING TITHE

Nothing is known about the antecedents or descendants of Melchisedec, and yet the known details of him show that he was the King of righteousness and King of peace, who received Tithe from the Patriarch Abraham and blessed him. Unless someone is superior to the other the one cannot receive Tithe from the latter nor can one bless the other. Melchisedec was the priest who lives forever continually with neither any beginning to his days nor any end.

Melchisedec who received Tithe from Abraham, was not a descendant of Abraham, while the Levites who received the Tithe were the descendants of Abraham. The descendants of Patriarch Abraham were Isaac, Jacob and his twelve sons. God said to Moses to appoint Aaron, from the Levite Tribe to be the high priest to serve in the Tabernacle. They received Tithes from people, and they paid their fair share of Tithe to God according to the Law of Moses given to the children of Israel.

In this sense Abraham paid the Tithe to Melchisedec on behalf of even those who were yet to be born, and those who were yet to be born were Aaron and his descendants. The Levite Tribe was in the seed of Abraham when he paid Tithe to Melchisedec, a priest who had no end of his days, while Aaron, and every priest of the descendant of Aaron died.

Even as Melchisedec had no end of days and not from Aaronic order of priests, received Tithe from the Patriarch Abraham, and blessed him, Lord Jesus Christ was not from the Tribe of Levi, the priests, but he was from the tribe of Judah, and from the lineage of David. That is why He was called the 'Son of God' and "Son of David".

CHAPTER 7

THE SON OF GOD

Lord Jesus was born of Virgin Mary as a result of the Holy Spirit coming upon her and the power of the Almighty overshadowed her. Thus the Holy Child Jesus was born of her even before she was united with Joseph, to whom she was espoused. Therefore, the Lord was called the "Son of God" (cf. Luke 1:35), and also as the "Son of David" according to the lineage (cf. Matt. 1:1; 1:20; Luke 1:32).

"And the angel answered and said unto her, The Holy Ghost shall come upon thee, and the power of the Highest shall overshadow thee: therefore also that holy thing which shall be born of thee shall be called the Son of God" (Luke 1:35).

HIS PRIESTHOOD

Inasmuch as Aaronic priesthood was not everlasting, and had deficiency it was done away with to be replaced by the everlasting priesthood of Lord Jesus Christ, who died on behalf of sinners, thus becoming a Mediator between God and man, and offering Himself as sacrifice unlike the Aaronic priesthood who offered animals as sacrifice even for them first and then for the people.

The priesthood of Lord Jesus Christ is, therefore, become perfect and everlasting, superior to the priest hood of Aaronic priesthood. It is, therefore, the priesthood of Lord Jesus Christ is greater than the priesthood of Aaron and his descendants, who were from the designated Levite tribe. Lord Jesus Christ is of the order of Melchisedec, of whom Moses did not say even a word, and thus He is the high priest forever and ever for Jews even as He is to the Gentile coverts to Christianity.

The curtain in the Temple was torn from top to bottom when Lord Jesus was crucified on the cross, thus removing barrier between Jews and Gentiles. He is the savior of the world, to the Jews and Gentiles alike, which was in accordance with the revelation made known to Simeon, and to Apostle Paul (Ref. Luke 2:25-32; 2:34; Ephesians 3:3-6).

It is obvious from all this that the Law only pointed sin in man, but never redeemed anyone from punishment that was associated with the transgression of it. The Mosaic Law made nothing perfect. However, Lord Jesus Christ, who arose as another priest not after the law of carnal commandment, but after the power everlasting life.

SWORN BY OATH

The Lord brought to us a better hope, by which we draw near to the Father. Aaron and his descendants were priests who were not confirmed by an oath by God. They received their priesthood when they reached certain age worthy of serving as priests and by their descent from Levitical priesthood, whereas Lord Jesus Christ became high priest for us by an oath.

Psalmist prophesied about Lord Jesus Christ when he said "thou art a priest forever after the order of Melchisedec" (cf. Psalm 110:4)

"The LORD hath sworn, and will not repent, Thou art a priest forever after the order of Melchizedek" (Psalms 110:4)

That is how Lord Jesus Christ fulfilled the Law on behalf of us and made us free from the bondage of the restrictions of the Mosaic Law. The weakness and un-profitableness of the Mosaic Law was disannulled; thus making the Lord high priest forever after the order of Melchisedec.

OF THE ORDER OF MELCHISEDEC

The priesthood now does not change but rests in Him and in Him alone. He being the brightness of the Father's glory and His express image of His person, upholds all things by the word of His power. He purged our sins and sat down on the right hand of the Majesty. He, who is "holy, harmless, undefiled, separate from sinners, and made higher than heavens" is interceding and pleading on behalf of us continually. That is the reason why He is able to save those who approach the Father by Him.

Unlike the Law of Moses, which made high priests by their descent from the Levites, who had infirmity in themselves, Lord Jesus Christ was made the high priest by the word of the oath; which was since the law that consecrated Him for the service as high priest and mediator between God and man. There is, therefore, no other priest either in this world or in heavens, than Lord Jesus Christ.

The Lord neither needed sacrifices for Himself, just as priest from Levitical Tribe needed to offer sacrifices for himself first before he did on behalf of others, nor does He need any more even as He is seated at the right hand of the Majesty rendering continuously the responsibility of interceding on behalf of us in the heavenly sanctuary, of which was the Tabernacle a shadow where priests rendered sacrifices and oblations.

The Lord offered His own body and precious blood once and for all not for Himself but on behalf of all sinners; thus providing way for anyone to accept Him as Savior and be forgiven of one's sin and receive everlasting life to be with Him forever and ever (cf. Hebrews 7:1-28)

CHAPTER 8

WHY SACRIFICES?

Biblical definition[1] of SACRIFICE is:

SAC'RIFICE, v.t. sac'rifize. L. sacrifico; sacer, sacred, and facio, to make.

1. To offer to God in homage or worship, by killing and consuming, as victims on an altar; to immolate, either as an atonement for sin, or to procure favor, or to express thankfulness; as, to sacrifice an ox or a lamb.
2. An offering made to God by killing and burning some animal upon an altar, as an acknowledgment of his power and providence, or to make atonement for sin, appease his wrath or conciliate his favor, or to express thankfulness for his benefits.

Biblical definition[2] of OBLATION is:

OBLA'TION, n. L. oblatio, from offero; ob and fero, to bear or bring.

Anything offered or presented in worship or sacred service; an offering; a sacrifice.

God chose Israel as His nation and the people of Israel as His people. He said He is their God and they are His people.

---

[1] Webster's Dictionary
[2] Webster's Dictionary

God delivered them from the bondage of slavery under Pharaoh in Egypt and led them to the Promised Land, Canaan, where, as the scripture says "milk and honey flow". On the same day they were delivered from Egypt, they travelled and crossed Red Sea and came to a place called "Rephidim" (cf. Exo.19:1-2). This is near the Mount Sinai, where God gave the Law in writing to the children of Israel by the hand of His servant Moses. The children of Israel left the premise of Mount Sinai in about one year. Here God desired to enter into a covenantal relationship with the children of Israel, but they quickly damaged their relationship by sinning against the LORD.

The children of Israel broke the Ten Commandments given to them. They worshipped Idol, a calf made of gold and bowing down to it as if it were their god. They soon forgot that the living God delivered them from their slavery which lasted for four hundred year slavery in Egypt. This was the reason why God said to Moses to instruct the children of Israel to build tabernacle, which was a portable structure.

It was at the entrance of the Tabernacle near Bronze Altar of the Tabernacle that the priests offered sacrifices. The priest attending the service applied the blood of the sacrifice on the horns of the altar and splattered rest of the blood of the sacrifice at the base of the altar.

The method of offering sacrifices differed depending upon the type of sacrifice that was offered. The high priest went into most holy place, once a year, to worship the LORD and atone for the people of Israel. The Tabernacle was moved from place to place as and when they moved to a new place during their forty years journey in the wilderness before they reached the Promised Land.

Offering sacrifices was a way of reconciliation of man with God and worship Him. God accepted their sacrifices for atonement of sin and received thanksgiving oblations from them. In order to come near God and worship Him they had to have their sin covered and become pure before they offered oblations.

They offered "Trespass offering" and "Sin offering" for atonement of their sins, as commanded by God. They offered "Burnt Offering" as their voluntary consecration to God, and thanksgiving, "Meal offering" as their service to God, and "Peace offering" as their fellowship offering as a token of having fellowship with God and fellowmen. The burnt offerings, meal offerings, peace offerings are considered as "Sweet-savor offerings" to the LORD because they do not denote sin in them. "Sin offerings" and the "Trespass offerings" are considered as "Non-savory offerings".

Basically there are only five kinds of offerings listed in sequentially in the book of Leviticus from Chapters 1 to 7 as follows:

1. BURNT OFFERING
2. MEAL OFFERING
3. PEACE OFFERING
4. SIN OFFERING
5. TRESPASS OFFERING

In addition, there are other offerings, which are subset of peace offerings.

They are:

- Thanksgiving Offering
- Wave Offering
- Votive offering

(cf. Leviticus 7:12-31)

CHAPTER 9

BURNT OFFERING

BURNT OFFERING - IMPORTANT POINTS IN TABULAR FORM

(Ref. Lev. 1:1-17; 6:8-13; 7:8; 8:18-21; 16:24

"Burnt offering" signifies the offeror's acknowledgement of his general guilt and its typical expiation. Except for the skin the entire offering is burnt on the altar. It signifies the offeror's voluntary consecration to God, in addition to his full devotion and his substance, as well.

OFFEROR AND PURPOSE	ELEMENTS USED AS SACRIFICE	SHARE OF THE SACRIFICE	BIBLE REFERENCES
Any man, who desires to offer voluntarily consecrating himself to God	Bullock or Male goat or sheep or Bird (pigeon or Dove)	Except for skin, entire sacrifice belongs to God. Skin belongs to the officiating priest	Ge 22:2-3,6-8,13; Ex 18:12; 29:18,25,42; 30:9,28; 31:9; 35:16; 38:1; Heb. 10:8

The origin of the Burnt offering is not in Leviticus but it was in Genesis. The burnt offering that Abel offered is considered as the first one but inasmuch as it was not offered on the altar, some consider Noah's burnt offering is the first one in the Bible. (cf. Genesis 4: 4; Genesis 8:20). Nevertheless, clear instructions from God to Moses, and the method of offering the Burnt offerings are found in the book of Leviticus.

The commandment to offer Burnt offering was given by God to the children of Israel by the mouth of Moses, His servant. The instructions are in Leviticus 1:1-17; 6:8-13; 7:8; 8:18-21; 16:24.

Depending on the affordability of a man, who offers Burnt offering to the LORD, he may choose bullock from the herd, or sheep or goat from the flock, or bird (a dove or pigeon) from the fowls of the air. The rich offered bullock, the poor offered sheep or goat and the poorest offered birds as burnt offering.

The LORD conveyed His commandment through His servant Moses to Aaron and his servants. The method by which they are to offer the Burnt offering is given by the LORD. It is the law of burnt offering and one should know the consequences of violating God's law.

The offering is called the Burnt offering because the offering is burnt upon the altar the entire night until the morning. It is the duty of the priests to oversee that the fire of the altar does not get extinguished.

THE CONDITIONS

IF THE ANIMAL IS FROM THE HERD:

- It should be a male without blemish

- The Burnt offering by man is voluntary
- It should be offered at the door of the Tabernacle
- The man offering Burnt offering should place his hands upon its head before the LORD
- The place is the north side of the altar.
- The offeror, (not the priest), shall kill the bullock before the LORD.
- The LORD will accept His offering as an atonement for him
- The LORD will accept the death of the animal as death in man's place
- The death of the animal in the place of sinner is the substitutionary death
- The priests, Aaron's sons, shall bring the blood and sprinkle it around the altar.
- The sprinkling of the blood around the altar is considered as the life of the man offered.
- The offeror peels off the skin of the animal and gives it to the priests for disposal
- The offeror then cuts the animal into pieces.
- The priests shall lay wood upon the altar and build a wood-fire
- They will place the pieces of the offering, other than skin, on the altar on the burning wood to be burnt
- The pieces will include the head of the animal and its fat. The Internal organs and the legs should be washed and placed on the altar
- The entire part of the animal thus placed on the altar shall be burnt

- This burning of all the parts except for the skin is called the "Burnt Offering"
- The burnt sacrifice is an offering made by fire, of a sweet savor unto the LORD and it is a pleasing aroma unto the LORD.

IF THE ANIMAL IS FROM THE FLOCK:

- If the animal that was to be presented it for burnt offering was from the flock, then it could be either a sheep or goat, but it must be male without any defect.
- The animal needs to be slaughtered on the north side of the altar in the LORD's presence. Aaron and his sons, who are priests should splatter its blood against all the sides of the altar.
- The animal, then needs to be cut into pieces. The priests will arrange the pieces of the offering including the head and fat on the wood on the altar.
- However, the internal organs and the legs should be first washed with water. Then the priest burns the entire sacrifice on the altar as a burnt offering. It is a special gift, a pleasing aroma to the LORD.

IF THE OFERING IS A BIRD.

- If a bird is presented as a burnt offering to the LORD, it could be either a turtledove or a young pigeon.
- The priest shall take the bird to the altar, wring off its head, and burn it on the altar. However, he must first drain its blood against the side of the altar.

- The priest shall remove the crop and the feathers and throw them in the ashes on the east side of the altar.
- The pries shall grasp the bird by its wings and will carefully tear the bird open so as to see that the bird is not torn apart. Then he burns it as a burnt offering on the wood burning on the altar. It is a special gift, a pleasing aroma to the LORD.

THE LAW OF BURNT OFFERING

- It is the duty of the priests to oversee that the fire of the altar does not get extinguished.
- During the entire time the burnt offering is on the altar until every act with regard to burnt offering is completed the priest is required to wear linen garment. His undergarments should be closely fastened to his body.
- The priest should remove the ashes of the burnt offering and put them beside the altar. He is not allowed to go elsewhere with the holy garments he had put on, and therefore, he shall remove those clothes and put on other garments and carry the ashes outside the camp to a clean place.
- In order that the fire never gets extinguished the priest shall add firewood every morning and shall burn upon the altar the fat of the peace (fellowship) offerings. The fire on the altar should be burning continuously and never go out (cf. Leviticus 6:8-13).

• IN THE CASE OF THE AARON AND HIS SONS

- When Aaron and his sons were anointed as priests, Aaron presented the ram for the burnt offering. He and his sons laid their hands on its head. Then Moses killed the ram and sprinkled the blood upon the altar round about. He cut the ram into pieces and burned the head and the pieces of the fat. He washed the entrails and the legs with water and burned the whole ram on the altar. It was burnt offering, a pleasing aroma, a food offering made by fire unto Jehovah. This was done as the LORD commanded Moses. (cf. Lev. 8:18-21)
- The high priestly service that was done once a year is described in Leviticus 16:1-28, more so in Leviticus 16:24 about the Burnt offering, where it says the high priest shall bathe himself with water in the sanctuary area and put on his regular clothes. Then he shall come out and offer his burnt sacrifice and then of the people, and make an atonement for himself and for the people.

CHAPTER 10

GRAIN OFFERING

"GRAIN OFFERING" (ALSO CALLAED "MEAL OFFERING" OR AS "MEAT OFFERING" - IMPORTANT POINTS IN TABULAR FORM

(Ref: Lev 2:1-16; 6:14-23)

OFFERER AND PURPOSE	ELEMENTS USED AS SACRIFICE	SHARE OF THE SACRIFICE	BIBLE REFERENCES
"Meal offering (also called Grain offering or "Meat Offering") is offered by the one who wishes to thank God voluntarily and to recognize God's goodness to him.	Grain, Fine Flour, Olive Oil, incense, baked cakes of bread or wafers, salt. No honey and no yeast	If it offered by priest, entire portion belongs to God If it is offered by anyone other than priest, handful belongs to God and rest of the offering belongs to the priest, who will eat the entire portion within the court of the Tabernacle.	Ex 29:41; 30:9; 40:29; Le 2:1,3-11,13-15; 5:13; 6:14-15,20-21,23; 7:9-10,37; 9:4,17; 10:12; 14:10,20-21,31; 23:13,16,18,37; Nu 4:16; 6:15,17; 7:13,19,25,31,37,43,49,55,61,67,73,79,87;

- It could be offered by anyone. However, it should be overseen by the sons of Aaron.
- It is a voluntary offering. It is an "Oblation", i.e. it is an offering presented to the LORD to worship Him. It is a sacred service and it is a sacrifice.
- Three elements are required for this offering: 1 finest flour, 2. Olive Oil, and 3. Frankincense. It shall be of fine flour with oil poured upon it and frankincense put on it.
- The man offering cannot directly take it to the altar; but it shall be brought to Aaron's sons the priests.
- The priest shall take from it, his handful of the flour thereof, and of the oil thereof, with all the frankincense thereof and burn it as a memorial portion on the altar.
- It is to the LORD, a food offering made by fire, a sweet savor, an aroma pleasing to the LORD.
- The remnant of the meat offering shall belong to Aaron and his sons.
- It is a most holy of the offerings of the LORD made by fire.

IF THE GRAIN OFFERING IS BAKED

- If anyone brings an oblation of grain offering baked in the oven it shall be of unleavened bread made of finest flour.
- It could be of either thick loaves made without yeast and with olive oil mixed in, or
- It could be of thin loaves made without yeast and brushed with olive oil.

IF THE GRAIN OFFERING IS PREPARED ON A GRIDDLE

- It should be made of the finest flour mixed with oil, and without yeast, crumbled it and with olive oil poured upon it.

IF THE GRAIN OFFERING IS COOKED IN A PAN

- If the grain offering is cooked in a frying pan, it should be made of finest flour and some olive oil.

IMPORTANT POINT

The grain offering intended to be offered to the LORD, should be presented to the priest, who will take to the altar. He shall take out handful of the offering, which is the memorial portion from the offering and burn it to the LORD on the altar as a food offering. It is an offering made by fire to the LORD and, therefore, is an aroma, a sweet savor pleasing to the LORD.

The rest of the grain offering belongs to Aaron and his sons. It is a most holy part of the food offerings presented to the LORD.

No grain offering intended to be offered to the LORD should ever be made with yeast or honey. The grain offering could be brought by man to the LORD as an offering of the first-fruits, but such offering (intended as first-fruits) should not be burnt on the altar as a pleasing aroma.

All the grain offerings should be seasoned with salt. Adding salt is very important because it represents the covenant of the LORD. Never should salt be left out of the grain offering.

The grain offering intended to be presented to the LORD as the first-fruits, should be of crushed heads of new grain roasted in the fire. Olive oil and incense should be put on it. The priest will burn the memorial portion of the crushed grain and the oil together with the entire incense on the altar as a food offering presented to the LORD. (Memorial portion is the handful of the offering from the total portion of the grain offering).

CHAPTER 11

PEACE OFFERING

(Ref: Lev 3:1-17; 7:11-34)

PEACE OFFERING (ALSO KNOWN AS "FELLOWSHIP OFFERING") " - IMPORTANT POINTS IN TABULAR FORM

OFFERER AND PURPOSE	ELEMENTS USED AS SACRIFICE	SHARE OF THE SACRIFICE	BIBLE REFERENCES
It is an offering made by the one who intends to thank God, worship Him, and have fellowship with others, in addition to having fellowship with God.	Animal without any blemish from either herd or from flock, and any variety of breads.	To God belong fatty portions such as fat covering inner parts, fatty tail, lobe of the liver and kidneys. To high priest belongs the breast. To officiating priest belongs right fore-leg. To the offeror belongs the remainder. Any left over until third day should be burnt;	Ex 29:28; Le 3:1,3,6,9; 4:10; 6:12; 7:13-14,32,37; 9:4,22; 22:21; 23:19; Nu 6:14,17; 7:17,23,29, 35,41,47,53 ,59,65,71,7 7,83; Eze 45:15,17; 46:2,12

		otherwise, whole purpose of peace offering gets defeated.	

POINTS

- If anyone's oblation is a sacrifice of peace offering, then he shall offer the animal male or female from the herd.
- The animal that is without any defect should be presented before the LORD
- He shall lay his hand upon the head of his offering and kill it at the entrance of the Tabernacle.
- Aaron's sons (the priests) shall sprinkle the blood upon the altar round about.
- He shall offer of the sacrifice of the peace offering.
- It will be an offering made by fire unto the LORD.
- The fat that covers the inward parts of the animal, and the entire fat that is upon it, with two kidneys, and the fat that is on them, which is by the flanks, and the caul above the liver, with kidneys be taken away.
- Aaron's sons shall burn that on the altar upon the burnt sacrifice, which is upon the wood that is on the fire.
- It is an offering made by fire, of a sweet savor unto the LORD.

CHAPTER 12

SIN OFFERING

It is about the sin committed unintentionally and does that which is forbidden by the LORD. (cf. Leviticus 4:1-35)

- It is about the priest who may sin and bring guilt upon the people
- Then, the priest shall bring to the LORD a young bullock without blemish
- The bullock should be brought to the entrance of the Tabernacle
- The sinner should place his hands on the head of the bullock and kill it there before the LORD
- The anointed priest shall take some of the bull's blood and carry into the Tabernacle
- The priest should dip his finger into the blood and splatter some of it seven times before the LORD before the veil of the sanctuary
- The priest shall then apply some of the blood on the horns of the altar of sweet incense before the LORD inside the Tabernacle.
- The priest shall then come out of the sanctuary and take the rest of the blood of the bull and shall pour out at the base of the bronze altar of burnt offering at the entrance of the Tabernacle
- The priest shall remove the entire fat from the bull of the sin offering, and the fat that connects internal organs one to another.
- He shall remove both the kidneys with the fat on them, and the long lobe of the liver

SIN OFFERING - IMPORTANT POINTS IN TABULAR FORM

OFFERER AND PURPOSE	ELEMENTS USED AS SACRIFICE	SHARE OF THE SACRIFICE	BIBLE REFERENCES
(1)Sin offering is made by priest on behalf of sinner. It includes high priest.	**In the case of high priest for his own sin** and for the people of Israel a bullock is to be offered	**To God:** All fatty portions of inner parts of the body – fat on the liver lob, fat on the kidneys, fatty tail	References: Ex 29:14,36; 30:10; Le 4:3,8,20-21,23-25,28-29,32-34; 5:6-13,15; 6:17,25,30;
(2) Sin offering is made by high priest on behalf of people of Israel.	**In the case of leader** a male goat is offered	**To the high priest:** If the atonement is for the high priest, his portion of the sacrifice is nothing. The entire remainder should be burnt outside the Tabernacle, where the ashes were thrown.	7:7,37; 8:2,14; 9:2-3,7-8,10,15,22; 10:16-17,19; 12:6,8; 14:13,19,22,31; 15:15,30; 16:3,5-6,9,11,15,25,27; 19:22; 23:19;
	In the case of common man a female goat or female lamb is offered		Nu 6:11,14,16; 7:16,22,28,34,40,16,52,58,64,70,76,82,87;
(3) Sin offering is mandatory for all who sin unintentionally, and later comes to know about it		**To the high priest if the atonement is made on behalf of others.** The entire remainder belongs to the high priest, who shall eat it within the	8:8,12; 9:13; 15:24-25,27; 18:9; 28:15,22; 29:5,11,16,19,22,25,28,31,34,38; 1Sa 2:17; 2Ch 29:21,23-
	In the case of poor a dove or pigeon is to be offered		

	In the case of very poor: One Tenth of an ephah of fine flour	Tabernacle. **To the offeror of the sin offering. Nothing belongs to him.**	24; Ezra 6:17; 8:35; Ne 10:33; Ps 40:6; Isa 53:10; Heb 10:8,18

- The priest shall burn the entire portion that was removed from the bull.
- However, the hide of the bull and entire flesh there from, and the head and legs, the entrails of the bullock, and the intestines, should be taken outside the camp to a clean place, where the ashes are thrown and burn it there in a wood fire on the ash heap.

CHAPTER 13

TRESSPASS OFFERING

- The "Trespass offering" is to be offered when anyone trespasses against the Law of the LORD and lies to his neighbor and deceives him of matters related to financial deposits or security breaches or gains through robbery,
- Or if he has oppressed his neighbor or lies about something that was lost and he found it, or swore falsely in any of those things that people do and sin thereby,
- If he has sinned and has realized his guilt and restores that which he took by robbery or that which he got by oppression, or guilty of the deposits that he failed to make, or lost that which he found, or anything that which he swore falsely, then
- He shall restore that which he has taken by robbery, or what he got by oppression or the deposit and add to it fifth of it (20% penalty) and give it to him on the day he realizes to whom it belongs.
- He shall bring to the priest as his compensation to the LORD a ram without blemish out of the flock or its equivalent for a guilt offering.
- The priest shall make atonement for him before the LORD, and he shall be forgiven for any of the things that one may do and thereby becomes guilty.
- The trespass offering that he has to make should be by compensating to the LORD a ram without blemish out of the flock or its equivalent, for a guilt offering.

- The priest shall make atonement for him before the LORD.
- Then, the LORD will mercifully forgive the offender from becoming guilty of the offences he committed.

TRESPASS OFFERING – IMPORTANT POINTS IN TABULAR FORM

OFFERER AND PURPOSE	ELEMENTS USED AS SACRIFICE	SHARE OF THE SACRIFICE	BIBLE REFERENCES
Trespass offering is by the one who commits sin willfully and with knowledge that he is sinning. Trespass offering is mandatory. It is an atonement for intentional. It requires restitution,	A ram without any blemish. The Law for Sin Offering and Trespass offering is same.	To God belongs Fatty portions. The Fat tail, the fat covering entrails of the animal, Kidneys and the lobe of the liver. Priest gets the remainder of the animal, which he has to eat within the Tabernacle. Offeror gets nothing.	References: Le 5:6-7,15-16,18-19; 6:5-6,17; 7:1-2,5,7,37; 14:12-14,17,21,24-25,28; 19:21-22; Nu 6:12; 18:9; 1Sa 6:3-4,8,17; Eze 40:39; 42:13; 44:29; 46:20

cleansing from defilement and payment of 20% penalty.			

THE LAW OF THE TRESSPASS OFFERING

- The law of the trespass offering is most holy of all the offerings. It should be offered at the place where burnt offering is offered. Thus the place where burnt offering and trespass offering is offered is at the entrance of the Tabernacle before the LORD on the bronze altar.
- The blood of the sacrifice should be sprinkled around the altar.
- The offeror should offer the entire fat including that which covers the entrails and also the rump (the end portion of the backbone of an animal with other parts adjacent to it. Jews considered the rump as the most delicate part of the animal).
- Along with these he should also offer the two kidneys of the animal and the fat which is on them by the flanks (the side portion between the ribs and the hip of the animal), and caul (the amniotic membrane that encloses fetus), which is above the liver.
- The priest shall burn them upon the altar for an offering made by fire unto the LORD.
- It is a trespass offering. Every male among the priests shall eat thereof.

- It should be eaten in the holy place. It is most holy offering
- There is one law for sin offering and trespass offering because the offering made for sin offering and trespass offering is similar to each other.
- The priest, who makes atonement with these offerings shall have this offering.
- The priest who makes burnt offering will have for himself the skin of the burnt offering that he has offered
- The entire grain offering which is baked in the oven, and the entire offering that is dressed in the frying pan and in the pan will be the portion of the priest, who offers it.
- Every meal offering, mixed with oil will be the portion of the sons of Aaron one as much as the other.
- Unlike as in peace offerings where the offeror shared the communion of God in Christ, here in sin offering and trespass offering the offeror had no share of the offering because he was confessing his sin before the LORD. It was shared between the altar and the priests.

(Ref. Leviticus 7:1-10)

SACRIFICES AND OBLATIONS		
WAVE OFFERING, HEAVE OFFERING AND FREEWILL OFFERING **WHO OFFERS AND PURPOSE** **ELEMENTS USED AS OFFERING** **WHO HAS THE SHARE OF THE OFFERING** **AND BIBLE REFERENCES**		
Definition of "SHEAF"	A quantity of the stalks of wheat, rye, oats or barley bound together; a bundle of stalks or straw.	
WAVE OFFERING AND HEAVE OFFERING They are offerings set apart for God. They are "exalted" and "lifted up" for God.	WAVE OFFERING AND HEAVE OFFERING ARE PART OF PEACE OF OFFERINGS. They are not separate offerings. Wave offering could be an animal or a sheaf. Waving of an offering sideways (left and right) by the priest before the altar is "WAVE OFERING". Waving of an	REFERENCES: Wave Offering: Ex 29:24,26-27; Le 7:30; 8:27,29; 9:21; 10:15; 14:12,24; 23:12,15,20; Nu 5:25; 6:20; 8:11; 18:11 Heave Offering: Ex 25:2-3; 29:27-28; Le 7:14,32; 10:15; Nu 5:9; 6:20; 15:19-21; 18:11,24,26-29; 31:29,41,52; De 12:11,17

	offering with an upward motion and downward motion by the priest before the altar is 'HEAVE OFFERING.	

FREEWILL OFFERINGS		
OFFERER AND PURPOSE	WHO HAS THE SHARE	HOW IT IS CONSUMED
Freewill offerings could be to fulfill a vow or a voluntary offering.	Breast of the wave offering is for the priest.	The entire remainder of the sacrifice should be eaten on the first day. No leftover, to the third day, is allowed. Entire leftover should be burnt; otherwise the whole purpose of the offering is defeated and it is considered as null and void. It is not honored by God and considered as an illegitimate offering.

REFERENCES: Exo. 29:27-28; Lev. 7:16-17; Lev. 23:12; Lev. 23:15		

=================

PEACE OFFERING

The sacrifice can be of any animal without defect from either herd or flock. In the case of vegetarian, it can be of variety of breads. It is a voluntary act of worship, thanksgiving and fellowship, which includes a meal for the community.

PARTS OF THE PEACE OFFERING

Fatty portions belong to God. Fatty portions include the covering of entrails of the animal, fat tail, kidney, and lobe of the liver.

Breast is given to the High Priest, who shall wave the offering before the LORD.

Right foreleg is given to the officiating priest. This offering is called 'heave offering'.

If it is "Thanksgiving offering": The entire remainder of the sacrifice has to be eaten on the first day and second day. No leftover is allowed.

If it is a "Vow of freewill offering": The entire remainder of the sacrifice should be eaten on the first day. No leftover, to the third day, is allowed. Entire leftover should be burnt; otherwise the whole purpose of the offering is defeated and it is considered as null and void. It is not honored by God and considered as an illegitimate offering.

"But if the sacrifice of his offering be a vow, or a voluntary offering, it shall be eaten the same day that he offereth his sacrifice: and on the morrow also the remainder of it shall be eaten: But the remainder of the flesh of the sacrifice on the third day shall be burnt with fire" (Leviticus 7:16-17)

"And ye shall offer that day when ye wave the sheaf an he lamb without blemish of the first year for a burnt offering unto the LORD" (Leviticus 23:12)

"And ye shall count unto you from the morrow after the sabbath, from the day that ye brought the sheaf of the wave offering; seven sabbaths shall be complete" (Leviticus 23:15)

CHAPTER 14

ANOINTING FOR GOD'S SERVICE

God said to Moses to take Aaron and his sons with him, and their garments, the anointing oil, and a bullock for sin offering and two rams for Burnt offering and a basket of unleavened bread for Grain offering to the entrance of Tabernacle where the children of Israel should have been assembled by then. As for the Grain offering, the basket should have bread made without yeast, think sheets of sweet bread mixed with oil, and unleavened wafers with oil poured over them; the bread made of fine ground wheat flour (cf. Exodus 29:1-3).

It is interesting to note that even though Moses was mediator between the children of Israel and God, he never did priestly service as Aaron and his sons did; nevertheless, the anointing of Aaron and his sons, and overseeing of their sin offering and burnt offering, was done by Moses (cf. Exodus 25-27; 40:34-35)

It is also interesting to note that Moses poured oil over the head of Aaron, but when it comes to sanctifying the sons of Moses, scriptures do not say that Moses poured oil over the heads of Aaron's sons. However, after the burnt offering is offered, Moses sprinkles the blood on Aaron, and his garments as also on Aaron's sons and their garments (cf. Exodus 29:21; Leviticus 8:30).

Moses said to the congregation that this entire ordination was being done according to the command of the LORD. He brought Aaron and his sons and washed them with water at the entrance of the Tabernacle. He then put upon Aaron the robe and tied it with the sash around him. He clothed him with robe and put upon it an ephod (sleeveless shirt) and girded it with girdle (a belt or cord worn around the waist), breastplate and in it "Urim" and "Thummim", which are a kind of ornaments that helped the high priest to give oracular answers to the people.

Moses then put upon the head of Aaron, the miter (tall headdress tapering to a point at front and back with deep cleft between, as symbol of office), and a gold plate, which is a sacred emblem, as the LORD commanded.

The earthly robe on the high priest helps us to ponder on the glorious and excellent robe that Lord Jesus Christ had on him, in resurrected body, as seen by John in his vision (Ref. Revelation 1:12-16)

Moses was commanded by God to take anointing oil and first anoint the tabernacle and every vessel and other items that was therein. Moses did as God commanded him to do and sanctified them. He then, as the LORD commanded him to do, poured anointing oil upon Aaron's head, thus anointed him as the high priest and sanctified him(cf. Leviticus 8:10-12).

As for the sons of Aaron who were priests Moses was commanded to dress them in their robes with woven sashes and caps placed on their heads. That was enough to be considered as having been commissioned as priests forever and they shall thus be consecrated.

A point to note here is that Aaron offered sin offering and burnt offering after he was anointed as high priest and his sons as priests, not vice versa.

CHAPTER 15

ANOINTING AARON AND HIS SONS

This is the order of anointing and consecration of Aaron as the high priest and his sons as the priests for God's service. It was a service that needs to be done only by the Aaron and his sons and their descendants from the tribe of Levi.

The ceremony for the dedication of Aaron and his sons as priests is narrated in Exodus 29:1-46 and Leviticus 8:1-36

Although Aaron and his sons were designated and appointed as priests, yet one thing was sure that they were human beings. They were born from the lineage of Adam and Eve and from the Levite Tribe, which was one of the twelve tribes of Israelites, the children of Jacob, who was called as "Israel" by the Almighty God Jehovah. Jacob was the grandson of Abraham, who was blessed by God and his offspring Isaac and Jacob are chosen generation, a peculiar people of God, and a nation chosen by God.

Except for Lord Jesus Christ, who was born from above in the womb of Virgin Mary when the Holy Spirit overshadowed on her, all mankind from Adam onwards, every single one of us, are sinners by virtue of Adam's original sin of transgressing the command of God.

Thus the entire offspring Adam to Levitical priesthood had imputation of original sin to them, and therefore, even though Aaron was chosen as high priest and his sons were chosen as priests they had to offer sacrifices for themselves first and then for the people of Israel.

None of these sacrifices are applicable to other nations, who were called as Gentile Nations. The Tabernacle was set up according to the command of God and specifications in the wilderness while the children of Israel were on their journey from Egypt to the Promised Land (cf. Exodus chapters 25 to 27). After the Tabernacle was set up, the glory of the LORD moved into the Tabernacle and the cloud covered the Tent of Meeting. Moses was not able to enter the Tabernacle.

"Then a cloud covered the tent of the congregation, and the glory of the LORD filled the tabernacle. And Moses was not able to enter into the tent of the congregation, because the cloud abode thereon, and the glory of the LORD filled the tabernacle" *(Exodus 40:34-35)*

After the children of Israel were redeemed from the bondage of slavery under Pharaoh of Egypt, they travelled from Egypt and crossed the Red Sea and came to Mount Sinai, where they spent nearly a year receiving the law and instructions from God through Moses His servant. That included the Instructions as to how to set up Tabernacle also (cf. Exodus 19:1-2).

Tabernacle was a portable structure set up in the wilderness for worshipping God the Almighty and seek his instructions. The children of Israel commenced journey first from Mount Sinai and then from place to place as and when the cloud was lifted by God from above the Tabernacle and started moving.

"On the twentieth day of the second month of the second year, the cloud lifted from above the tabernacle of the covenant law. Then the Israelites set out from the Desert of Sinai and traveled from place to place until the cloud came to rest in the Desert of Paran. They set out, this first time, at the LORD's command through Moses" Numbers 10:11-13

The children of Israel wrapped the portable tent along with all the elements therein and carried by hand by the designated people from one place to the other. The designated people who carried the all the elements of Tabernacle from place to place were sons of Gershon and the Sons of Merari (cf. Numbers 10:17)

They stopped at the next place as God desired and until next move was indicated by God they all stayed at that place and set up the Tabernacle again. They started moving again and repeated the sequences in all their forty years of wilderness journey until they reached the Promised Land.

Inasmuch as the Levites who were chosen also had sin in them, they had to offer sacrifices for themselves first and then for the people. When it came to Lord Jesus Christ, He was perfect "Lamb of God" without any blemish, and therefore, He had no necessity to offer sacrifice for Himself first and then for the people.

SIN OFFERING BY AARON AND HIS SONS

- In the presence of Moses and as the LORD commanded Aaron brought the bullock, which was without blemish, to offer it as sin offering on behalf of himself and his sons. Aaron and his sons placed their hands on the bullock's head for sin offering and the bullock was killed by Aaron.
- Moses took the blood and applied it, with his finger on the horns of the brazen altar, purifying it, at the entrance of the Tabernacle within the outer court.
- Thereafter, he poured it at the bottom of the altar and sanctified it in order to make reconciliation upon it.
- He took the entire fat that was upon the entrails of the slain bullock, i.e., the fat that was on the caul above the liver, and that was upon the two kidneys, and burnt it upon the altar.
- However, he did not burn the entire bullock on the altar as the LORD commanded.
- He took rest of the portions of the bullock, i.e. the hide, the flesh, the dung, and burnt it with fire outside the camp as the LORD commanded Moses.
- After that was done, that is after offering the sin offering, Aaron brought the first ram for burnt offering. Notice burnt offering followed sin offering. Burnt offering can also be offered independent of sin offering or trespass offering. However sin offering needs inevitably followed by burnt offering.
- Aaron and his sons placed their hands on the ram's head, and Aaron killed the first ram.
- Moses took the blood and sprinkled it upon the altar round about.
- Moses cut the ram into pieces.

- Moses burnt the head of the ram, and the rest of the pieces, and the fat.
- He washed the entrails of the ram, and its legs with water, and burnt the whole ram upon the altar.
- The slain ram was burnt upon the altar as the LORD commanded Moses and it was a sweet savor, an offering made by fire unto the LORD.
- Sin offering and Trespass offerings are non-sweet savor offerings, while the burnt offering, Grain offering and peace offering are sweet smelling savor unto the LORD.
- After the burnt offering was offered, Aaron brought the second ram, which was the ram of consecration.
- Aaron and his sons placed their hands on the second ram's head, and the ram was killed by Aaron.
- Moses took the blood of the ram and applied it upon the tip of Aaron's right ear, and upon his thumb of the right hand, and upon the great toe of his foot.
- Moses sprinkled the blood on the altar and around it.
- He took the fat and the rump (the end part of the backbone with parts adjacent to it) along with the entire fat that was on the entrails of the ram, i.e. the fat from the caul above the liver, and fat from the two kidneys, and the right shoulder.
- He also took one unleavened bread out of the many from the basket that was set before the LORD, and another oiled cake of the unleavened bread, and one wafer, and put them on the fat, and the right shoulder.
- Moses put this collection on Aaron's hands and on the hands of his sons, and waved them for a wave offering before the LORD.
- After the wave offering is over, Moses took this collection and burnt them on the altar upon the burnt offering.

- These were the consecrations to the LORD, a sweet savor, an offering made by fire unto the LORD.
- Then, Moses took the breast portion of the ram and waved it for a wave offering before the LORD, for ram of consecration. It was his share of the ordination, as the LORD commanded.
- The next part of the ceremony was to consecration of Aaron and his sons and the garments of Aaron and the garments of his sons.
- In order to do that Moses took some of the oil and some of the blood from the bronze altar and mixed oil and blood. He sprinkled this mixture of oil and blood on Aaron and his garments and likewise, on Aaron's sons and on the garments of his sons. Thus he commenced the ceremony of consecration which was to last for seven days. Aaron and his garments and his sons and their garments.
- Moses continued as God commanded and said to Aaron and his sons to boil the flesh of the ram at the door of the Tabernacle, and to eat it with the bread that was in the basket of consecration.
- Aaron and his were instructed to burn the rest of the flesh and of the bread with fire.
- Aaron and his sons were not to out of the door of the Tabernacle, but to stay and the entrance of the Tabernacle, for seven days until the completion of consecration.
- The consecration service was to be done for seven days.
- It was a very serious service ordered by the Almighty God; and any violation was surely to end up in death.
- The LORD commanded the anointing and consecration to last for seven days and they are to do that which the LORD required them to do; lest they should die. (Ref. Leviticus 8:1-36)

CHAPTER 16

ATONEMENT

"Also on the tenth day of this seventh month there shall be a day of atonement: it shall be an holy convocation unto you; and ye shall afflict your souls, and offer an offering made by fire unto the LORD" (Leviticus 23:27).

The "Day of Atonement" was celebrated by Israelites on the tenth day of seventh month as a memorial of the way the High Priest went into the "Holy of Holies" and sprinkled of the blood of the goat on which the lottery fell as "for the Lord" (Leviticus 16:8-9) and also as memorial of the second goat which was the "Scapegoat". The two goats collectively were the shadow of the sacrifice of Jesus on the cross and bearing the sins of the sinner.

"And Aaron shall cast lots upon the two goats; one lot for the LORD, and the other lot for the scapegoat" (Leviticus 16:8).

This is the sixth feast of the seven feasts described in Leviticus Chapter 23.

The great Day of Atonement was the shadow of the crucifixion of Lord Jesus Christ who died on behalf of us bearing our sin outside the gates of the city. Gospel writers Matthew, Mark, and John used the word "Golgotha", which means "place of skulls". Luke used the word "Calvary" instead of "Golgotha" and Calvary means "Cranium" which again means the same as "skull". (Matthew 27:33, Mark 15:22, Luke 23:33, John 19:17)

"For he hath made him to be sin for us, who knew no sin; that we might be made the righteousness of God in him" 2 Corinthians 5:21.

"And Aaron shall cast lots upon the two goats; one lot for the LORD, and the other lot for the scapegoat" (Leviticus 16:8 – KJV)

Darby's Translation of Leviticus 16:8 says: "And Aaron shall cast lots upon the two goats: one lot for Jehovah, and the other lot for Azazel".

The word "Azazel" is not clearly understood by any one. The most accepted meaning is the same as "Scapegoat", which bore the confessed sins and went into the wilderness and died, never to return to the camp of Israel. This "Scapegoat" is not Satan, which some believe it to be.

The "Scapegoat" is the picture of Lord Jesus Christ, who bore our sins. This is highly misunderstood doctrine in Christian Theology. Satan did not carry the sins of any one nor does any one need to lay one's sin on Satan to take away into wilderness. Some believe that it was Satan, who brought sin into the world and, therefore, Satan carries sin and dies in the wilderness, but this teaching is heresy.

Jesus died for our sins and he bore our sins and died on the outskirts of city. Jesus is the salvation and his blood cleansed our sins.

"For he hath made him to be sin for us, who knew no sin; that we might be made the righteousness of God in him" 2 Corinthians 5:21.

The sacrifices offered in the Old Testament period covered their sins, but they were not forgiven forever. They had to do it again the next year. In the New Testament period we are privileged that we do not need to offer such sacrifices repeatedly. Christ died for our sake once and for all; and that was enough. Our part is to believe Jesus as our Savior and repent of our sins to him. Jesus is the mediator for us and He is our High priest.

"But Christ being come an high priest of good things to come, by a greater and more perfect tabernacle, not made with hands, that is to say, not of this building; Neither by the blood of goats and calves, but by his own blood he entered in once into the holy place, having obtained eternal redemption for us" (Hebrews 9:11-12)

"So Christ was once offered to bear the sins of many; and unto them that look for him shall he appear the second time without sin unto salvation". (Hebrews 9:28)

The blood of Jesus Christ cleansed the sins of the Old Testament Saints, and also the New Testament saints. Lord Jesus became the High Priest, after the order of Melchisedec, thus setting aside the imperfect sacrificial offerings of the Old Testament. Jesus was the Savior in the past, He is the Savior now, and He will be the Savior in future. Hebrews Chapters 9, 10 and 11 detail the way Jesus became perfect sacrifice for all.

"But Christ being come an high priest of good things to come, by a greater and more perfect tabernacle, not made with hands, that is to say, not of this building; Neither by the blood of goats and calves, but by his own blood he entered in once into the holy place, having obtained eternal redemption for us" (Hebrews 9:11-12)

"So Christ was once offered to bear the sins of many; and unto them that look for him shall he appear the second time without sin unto salvation (Hebrews 9:28)

The blood of Jesus Christ cleansed the sins of the Old Testament Saints, and also the New Testament saints. Lord Jesus became the High Priest, after the order of Melchisedec, thus setting aside the imperfect sacrificial offerings of the Old Testament. Jesus was the Savior in the past, He is the Savior now, and He will be the Savior in future. Hebrews Chapters 9, 10 and 11 detail the way Jesus became perfect sacrifice for all.

CHAPTER 17

SACRIFICES IN THE NEW TESTAMENT

While the sacrifices in the Old Testament were physical, the sacrifices in the New Testament are Spiritual. : Lord Jesus Christ fulfilled the Law of Moses and became mediator between God and man. His sacrifice entailed repenting sinner to be reconciled to God.

Although He was sinless, yet He became sin for us, in order that we by accepting His as our savior, and by believing in heart that God raised Him from the dead would receive everlasting life to be in heaven with Him forever and ever.

It pleased the Father to bruise Him on the cross in order to provide a way for sinner to be reconciled to Him. We were enemies of God dead in trespasses; but while we were yet sinners Christ died for us. His crucifixion would have been of no avail if He did not rise from the dead. It is with boldness that can enter the presence of the Almighty God through the only mediator, who is Lord Jesus Christ, raised from the dead by God, on the third day His body did not corrupt when He was in the tomb. He has provided several witnesses of His resurrection that we may believe.

CHAPTER 18

THE WITNESSES

"And after this Joseph of Arimathaea, being a disciple of Jesus, but secretly for fear of the Jews, besought Pilate that he might take away the body of Jesus: and Pilate gave him leave. He came therefore, and took the body of Jesus. And there came also Nicodemus, which at the first came to Jesus by night, and brought a mixture of myrrh and aloes, about an hundred pound weight. Then took they the body of Jesus, and wound it in linen clothes with the spices, as the manner of the Jews is to bury" (John 19:38-40)

There were innumerable evidences at the crucifixion and resurrection of Lord Jesus Christ, and yet God provided us three sure witnesses, who were Government officials. Therefore, the contention over crucifixion of Jesus and His resurrection is of no validity.

In the verses quoted from John 19:38-40, and Matthew 27:54 it is so clear that Lord Jesus Christ was crucified in the presence of Joseph of Arimathaea, Nicodemus, and a very notable Centurion. Multitude of people from Jewish community, and from Gentile community cried saying "Crucify Him, Crucify Him", when the Lord was before Pontius Pilate for a trail.

Jesus was tried by the Roman Governor, Pontius Pilate, who after questioning the Lord, found no evidence of His violation of any edicts of Government. The Jews in those days had no power to punish anyone. Roman Government had seized the powers from them and the alleged victims had to be tried by the Government authority.

Therefore, Jews brought Lord Jesus before Pontius Pilate, the then Governor, who was a legal authority to try the alleged person and sentence him to death or similar punishment. The Jews knew that healing the diseased, casting our demons from the affected, raising the dead, and many other miracles done by Lord Jesus did not qualify for His death, but were only provided Him the credit of doing good to people. Truly, Lord Jesus did no harm to anyone during His life on this earth. He had done good and only good for the people. He had no sin in him, and there was without any blemish. Pilate, after trying Him to see if the Lord had transgression of any secular law of the regime, loudly proclaimed that Lord Jesus Christ was innocent. He did not deserve death, much less by crucifixion.

The Jews laid three allegations against Jesus knowing pretty well that only allegations pertaining to violation of Government edicts will result in His crucifixion. If the Lord were to be charged with allegation of healing the diseased, and such other good works He had done, Pilate would have instantly said to take Him away from the trial.

Seeing that Jews brought Jesus before Pilate for a trial and crucifixion, Pilate went out of the Judgment hall to question the High Priest Caiaphas, and the Jews, who stayed back from entering the judgment hall, lest it would have been against their moral ethics and violation of the Law of Moses.

The three charges the levelled by the multitudes of people against Jesus were that

1. He perverted the nation (treason and insurrection)
2. He forbade people from giving tribute to Caesar
3. He proclaimed that He is Christ a King.

All the three allegations they levelled against Jesus were false accusations.

1. Lord Jesus never gathered multitude for the sake of causing insurrection against Government. The crowds gathered around Him because He was doing miracles, the kind of which no one ever has done. The Lord even raised the dead, which was the greatest among other miracles He had done.

2. Lord Jesus never promoted rebellion or non-payment of taxes to the Government. Rather, He paid taxes, even though He being from above, not required to pay taxes. In Luke 20:21-25 the words of Lord Jesus are noteworthy. The chief priest and the scribes tried to catch Him in His words and asked Him a question. They asked Him if it was lawful for them to pay taxes to Caesar. However, the Lord perceived their craftiness said to them, "why tempt ye me? Show me a penny" and then went on asking them as to whose image and superscription was thereon. They answered and said that it was Caesar's. Then the Lord said to them, "Render therefore unto Caesar the things which be Caesar's, and unto God the things which be God's. (cf. Luke 20:21-25). Thus, it was very much evident that Lord Jesus never said to anyone not to pay taxes.

3. As to the third allegation, Pilate asked Him if He was he king of the Jews, Lord Jesus answered him saying "...Dost thou say this of thyself, or have others said it to thee concerning me?" (John 18:34) When Pilate's honesty was at stakes, he ventured justifying his question even though he heard that false accusation from the Jews. Pilate, in turn asked Jesus, Jesus "Am I a

Jew? Thy nation and the chief priests have delivered thee up to me: what hast thou done?" (John 18:35). Lord Jesus answered Him saying His kingdom was not of this world, and if it were of this word, then His followers would have fought for Him being delivered to the Jews for crucifixion.

It may be noted that when Peter, the disciple of Lord Jesus Christ, tried to fight for Jesus and cut off the ear of one named "Malchus" with his sword (cf. John 18:10), the Lord said to him, "Thinkest thou that I cannot now pray to my Father, and he shall presently give me more than twelve legions of angels?" (Matthew 26:53)

Interesting to note that Roman army was divided into legions and one legion was equivalent to six thousand men. Isaiah 39:36 records that single angel went out and killed 185000 men in one night. They were Sennacherib's army (not demons). According to that calculation 12 legions is equivalent to 72000. Now, if we calculate the numbers it goes like this... The Lord could call for twelve legions of angels. Thus, the combined strength is 72000 x185000 − 13,320,000,000 (That is equivalent to thirteen billion, three hundred twenty million men). Is it not amazing that Lord Jesus could call twice the number of people living on earth now? If so, what was that prevented Him doing that? It is because He wanted to save us from destruction. It was the Father's purpose that the Son should die one behalf of us. Yet it pleased the LORD to bruise him; he hath put him to grief: when thou shalt make his soul an offering for sin, he shall see his seed, he shall prolong his days, and the pleasure of the LORD shall prosper in his hand. (Isaiah 53:10)

Jesus said to Pilate that His kingdom was not of this world and if it were of this world then His servants would have fought for Him to prevent Him being delivered to the Jews. The Lord said to Pilate "Thou sayest that I am a king. To this end was I born, and for this cause came I into the world, that I should bear witness unto the truth. Every one that is of the truth heareth my voice".

Lord Jesus Christ was indeed the king of the Jews. When Jesus was born there was no room in the inn, and therefore, his earthly parents wrapped him in swaddling clothes and laid Him in a manger. This was to fulfill scriptures.

For he shall grow up before him as a tender plant, and as a root out of a dry ground: he hath no form nor comeliness; and when we shall see him, there is no beauty that we should desire him. He is despised and rejected of men; a man of sorrows, and acquainted with grief: and we hid as it were our faces from him; he was despised, and we esteemed him not. (Isaiah 53:2-3)

For unto us a child is born, unto us a son is given: and the government shall be upon his shoulder: and his name shall be called Wonderful, Counsellor, The mighty God, The everlasting Father, The Prince of Peace. (Isaiah 9:6)

Paul writes...

"But made himself of no reputation, and took upon him the form of a servant, and was made in the likeness of men" (Philippians 2:7)

Nevertheless, Lord Jesus was born king. Wise men, who came from the east to Jerusalem, inquired of Him, saying "...Where is he that is born King of the Jews? for we have seen his star in the east, and are come to worship him" (Matthew 2:1-2)

After Pilate asking rhetorical question as to what the truth was, he did not wait to receive a reply, but went out Judgment hall and spoke to waiting Jews and said to them that he did not find any guilt in Jesus. He declared Jesus as "not guilty". Yet, fearing the crows, who repeatedly cried "crucify him, crucify him", he delivered Jesus to them for crucifixion. They even preferred Barabbas, a noted criminal to be released than Jesus (cf. John 18:29-40).

"But they cried, saying, Crucify him, crucify him" (Luke 23:21)

According to tradition Roman Government released a prisoner at the Passover feast. Pilate asked if they desired to have Jesus released in preference over Barabbas, who was a notorious criminal, and who had resorted to insurrection and treason against Government, but alas! They preferred Barabbas in preference to that of Jesus and cried out loudly to crucify Jesus.

Notice how the Jewish nation has called upon themselves the curse of the innocent blood upon their children. They said "...His blood be on us, and on our children".

This calling upon themselves the curse did not go in vain. The Jewish nation has paid tremendously when they were killed mercilessly by Titus in 70 A.D. Jerusalem was destroyed and the whole nation is levelled to the ground.

Until recent times in 1948 A.D. the Jews suffered having been scattered among nations in the world and suffering greatly in those nations. It was by God's mercy that Israel has become a nation again on 18th April, 1948. Their language Hebrew is restored to them beyond one's imagination.

It was God's hand that helped them to come back to their land again. Nevertheless, the promises made by God to Abraham, about the restoration of the lands by their tribes is yet to happen and it will happen in one thousand years of reign of Lord Jesus Christ from the throne of David.

"When Pilate saw that 4he multitude, saying, I am innocent of the blood of this just person: see ye to it. Then answered all the people, and said, His blood be on us, and on our children" (Matthew 27:24-25)

SCARLET ROBE

The people sought the release of notorious criminal, who instigated insurrection of the Roman Government. They preferred his release over the innocent Jesus, who did only good and good, and never any bad for the people. It was all because of jealousy that the leaders of Jewish community that they wanted Jesus to be crucified. They levelled against Jesus, charges that never were proved. Pontius Pilate the governor of the land declared him innocent, and yet they cried aloud to crucify Him.

As if that was not enough, Pontius Pilate the governor of the land, ordered scourging of Jesus, in spite of declaring Him as innocent. It was just in contrast of the prevailing Roman laws, wherein if one is declared as innocent, he should never be scourged, Pilate chose to hand the Lord over to the Jews to be crucified, violating the laws of the country.

Roman Government's soldiers took custody of Jesus and after stripping him, put on Him a scarlet robe. The color scarlet indicates sin. Apostle Paul writes in 2 Corinthians 5:21 that the Lord, who knew no sin, was made sin for us, in order that we might by believing in Him, might be made the righteousness of God in Him.

"For he hath made him to be sin for us, who knew no sin; that we might be made the righteousness of God in him" (2 Corinthians 5:21)

More than seven hundred years before the crucifixion of Jesus Isaiah the prophet wrote that though our sins be as scarlet, yet they shall be made as white as snow, and though they be red like crimson, they shall be made as white as wool.

"Come now, and let us reason together, saith the LORD: though your sins be as scarlet, they shall be as white as snow; though they be red like crimson, they shall be as wool". (Isaiah 1:18)

Rahab the harlot, who helped Joshua's two spies, by faith that she would be delivered, when they come into the land of Canaan, escaped her death, by obeying Joshua's instructions, and tying a scarlet robe on her window. She did not perish along with those who did not believe. (cf. Joshua 2:1; Joshua 2:18; Joshua 6:25; Hebrews 11:31)

While Moses was confirming the Old Covenant spoke every precept to the people of Israel according to the law, and took blood of the calves and of goats, with water, and scarlet wool, and hyssop, sprinkled both the book and all the people (cf. Hebrews 9:19)

In Revelation 17:3-5 the woman is described on upon a scarlet colored beast that had on it, full of names of blasphemy, having seven heads and ten horns. This woman was arrayed in purple and scarlet color and "decked with gold and precious stones and pearls, having a golden cup in her hand full of abominations and filthiness of her fornication: And upon her forehead was a name written, MYSTERY, BABYLON THE GREAT, THE MOTHER OF HARLOTS AND ABOMINATIONS OF THE EARTH. (Revelation 17:3-5)

By stripping Jesus and putting on Him the scarlet robe, the soldiers and the people have equated Him to be a man of sin, although He was without any blemish, and without any sin in Him. He was made sin for us. He bore our shame, and He was crucified for our sake, in order that we might, by accepting Him as Lord, and by believing in His resurrection, receive everlasting life.

CROWN OF THORNS

Not only they insulted Lord Jesus by putting on Him scarlet robe, but they also put on His head a crown of thorns. It is of great interest to note that when God created the heavens, and earth, plants, animals, man and woman and everything that is in heaven, and on earth, and in seas, he never created the thorns. However, when man sinned against God, the LORD cursed the creation and it was then that the leaves on the plants turned into thorns, a consequential product. The thorns indicate curse, and it was this curse that Lord Jesus was bearing upon Himself, on our behalf in order that we may be redeemed of that curse.

"Christ hath redeemed us from the curse of the law, being made a curse for us: for it is written, Cursed is every one that hangeth on a tree" (Galatians 3:13)

REED

The soldiers and the people, then insulted Jesus by putting a reed in his right hand, and bowing before Him on their knees, and mocked Him, saying, *"Hail, King of the Jews! And they spit upon him, and took the reed, and smote him on the head. And after that they had mocked him, they took the robe off from him, and put his own raiment on him, and led him away to crucify him. And as they came out, they found a man of Cyrene, Simon by name: him they compelled to bear his cross"* (Matthew 27:26-32)

Lord Jesus Christ, the incarnate God, was born into this world in the form of a servant and in the likeness of man, relinquishing all the glory that He had with the Father in order to save sinners. He was from the tribe of Judah, of whom the prophecy in Genesis 49:10 reads...

The scepter shall not depart from Judah, nor a lawgiver from between his feet, until Shiloh come; and unto him shall the gathering of the people be. (Genesis 49:10)

Psalmist describes the power and the glory of the Lord in Psalm 45:6

"Thy throne, O God, is for ever and ever: the scepter of thy kingdom is a right scepter" (Psalms 45:6)

The writer of Hebrews quotes Psalmist's prophecy and says The Father gave the Son the honor and called Him God and said...

"But unto the Son he saith, Thy throne, O God, is for ever and ever: a scepter of righteousness is the scepter of thy kingdom". *(Hebrews 1:8)*

THE POWER OF THE SCEPTER

From the Old Testament book of Esther the power of the Scepter can be seen. Except in one circumstance, the law for disobeying and entering into King's inner circle by anyone, was sure death. Even Esther, who was King's wife, could not afford to take risk of entering into the inner circle of King, when he is in the midst of official business. The circumstance wherein the exemption was allowed was when king extends his scepter as a token of showing his permission to enter into the inner circle.

There arose an occasion when Esther had to enter into the inner circle of king when he was on his official business. Esther put on her royal apparel, and went into the inner court of the palace in front of the king's house. The king was on his royal throne in the royal house facing the entrance. The king saw Esther, and he was pleased to extend his golden scepter toward her, and she went and touched the tip of his scepter.

Here, urgency of the matter is seen, and in the midst of all risks, Esther went into the inner court of king to talk to him about important matter. The king accepted her and saved her from death penalty. The holding out of the scepter by the one, who had the authority to pardon an offence, and touching of the scepter by the one, who needed mercy, signified the offence, and the pardon that followed it.

In the case of sinner in the New Testament period, he, who needed mercy to be pardoned for his sin, has to approach Lord Jesus Christ, who had the authority to pardon. He has already held out his scepter towards all sinners, by offering Himself on the cross as a perfect sacrifice. (cf. Esther 4:11; 5:1, 2)

Alas! The soldiers and the people mocked Lord Jesus by putting in his hand a branch of aquatic plant as if it was the scepter that the scriptures spoke of. They mocked the Lord by bowing to Him, as if the aquatic branch was the Lord's scepter.

All those, who have mocked Him, and have not been pardoned by the Lord, will see the power of the scepter of the lion of Judah, Lord Jesus Christ, whose kingdom shall never come to an end. The Bible is clear that God cannot be mocked. Whoever mocks Lord Jesus Christ shall reap the consequences of doing so. Every knee will bow down to Him one day and accept Him as the Lord. It is good for one to accept Jesus as the Lord, before he is forced to kneel down to the Lord one day.

"Be not deceived; God is not mocked: for whatsoever a man soweth, that shall he also reap". (Galatians 6:7)

"That at the name of Jesus every knee should bow, of things in heaven, and things in earth, and things under the earth; And that every tongue should confess that Jesus Christ is Lord, to the glory of God the Father" (Philippians 2:10-11)

CHAPTER 19

THE EVIDENCES OF JESUS

Many people desire to know the proof of existence of Jesus, His crucifixion, burial and resurrection. God had taken care of these things very carefully in order that after crucifixion of Jesus, and His burial, resurrection and ascension, people may not call the realities as false stories.

John 19:38-40 corroborated with few other references gives us ample evidence which we may share with those who have doubts about these facts, and or on purpose propagate false stories against Him.

"And after this Joseph of Arimathaea, being a disciple of Jesus, but secretly for fear of the Jews, besought Pilate that he might take away the body of Jesus: and Pilate gave him leave. He came therefore, and took the body of Jesus. And there came also Nicodemus, which at the first came to Jesus by night, and brought a mixture of myrrh and aloes, about an hundred pound weight. Then took they the body of Jesus, and wound it in linen clothes with the spices, as the manner of the Jews is to bury" (John 19:38-40):

PROPHECIES FULFILLED

If only Satan knew that the death, burial and resurrection of Jesus Christ, perhaps, he would have put in all the skills and efforts he had at his disposal to prevent him being die on the cross rather than entering into the mind of Judas Iscariot and people to betray the Lord and seeking His crucifixion. Satan thought by putting the Lord to die on the cross he was gaining victory, but he failed in his purpose. On the other hand Scriptures say that it pleased the Father to bruise His only Son in order that we may find way to everlasting life. Jesus, who knew no sin became sin for us, and our sin was judged on the cross. He, who believes that Jesus is Lord and believes in heart that God raised Him from the dead will be saved.

People and Satan assigned grave for the Jesus but the Father took care of the Son in His death, whereby the prophecy in Isaiah 53:9 was fulfilled. No doubt, Jesus died outside the city, as it is written in the prophesies and in Hebrews 13:12

"And he made his grave with the wicked, and with the rich in his death; because he had done no violence, neither was any deceit in his mouth". (Isaiah 53:9)

Wherefore Jesus also, that he might sanctify the people with his own blood, suffered without the gate. (Hebrews 13:12)

Lord Jesus died in Golgotha (cf. Matthew 27:33), also called 'Calvary' (Luke 23:33), which was outside the gate in the midst of two malefactors, and was buried in the tomb that belonged to Joseph of Arimathaea, who was a rich man. The tomb was new and was located in a garden. Thus God gave Him place with the rich, even though He was crucified in the midst of two malefactors.

JOSEPH OF ARIMATHAEA

*"And, behold, there was a man named Joseph, a counsellor; and he was a good man, and a just: (The same had not consented to the counsel and deed of them) he was of Arimathaea, a city of the Jews: who also himself waited for the kingdom of God".
(Luke 23:50-51)*

"Joseph of Arimathaea, an honorable counsellor, which also waited for the kingdom of God, came, and went in boldly unto Pilate, and craved the body of Jesus". (Mark 15:43)

It takes courage and devotion on the part of someone who decides to give to someone else, his precious tomb built for his own burial. Joseph of Arimathaea was one such man, who was a counsellor, and a rich man secretly followed Jesus Christ. He patiently waited for the kingdom of God. After the crucifixion of Jesus, he went boldly to the governor, Pontius Pilate and craved for the Lord's body in order to bury His body in the tomb that he made for himself. He not only followed the Lord sincerely but his devotion and awe for the Lord exceeded any common man.

After Joseph of Arimathaea having received permission from the Pilate to take down the body of Lord Jesus, he took it down and wrapped the body in linen, according to the custom of erstwhile Jews. (Compare the death and burial of Lazarus, brother of Martha and Mary [John 11:19; 44]).

Joseph of Arimathaea wrapped in linen the body of Jesus and laid it in a sepulcher, wherein never any man's dead body was placed earlier. The sepulcher was hews in stone and was new and it was located in the garden near the crucifixion site.

"Now in the place where he was crucified there was a garden; and in the garden a new sepulchre, wherein was never man yet laid" (John 19:41)

In the meanwhile, as the Sabbath drew on after the preparation, the women, who came with Him from Galilee oversaw the sepulcher and observed the way the body of Jesus was laid in the new tomb of Joseph of Arimathaea. They laid the body in the tomb on the day of Passover, and they returned and prepared spices and ointments, and rested the Sabbath day according to the fourth commandment of the Ten Commandments (cf. Luke (Luke 23:52-56).

NICODEMUS

God's provision of another important evidence of the death of Jesus Christ is seen in the life of Nicodemus, who was a ruler of the Jews. He was the one, who was curious to know what it means to be born-again. As seen of his devotion to the Lord, it is evident that he too was a secret disciple of Jesus Christ.

The first mention of Nicodemus was about his visit to the Lord on a night and calling Him as "Rabbi", which means "teacher", and willing to learn as to what the Lord would speak to him. Nicodemus, who had great authority, and who was a ruler, was submissive to the Lord while inquiring as to how what it means to be born-again. Initially, he acknowledged that the Lord was a great teacher, who came from God; for no man could do such great miracles as the Lord did.

Lord Jesus was point blank to him and said to him that truly, truly unless a man is born again, he cannot see the kingdom of God. Nicodemus desired to know more about being born-again. Then, Lord Jesus explained to him that he hat is born of the flesh is of flesh, but he that is born of the Spirit is spirit. (John 3:1-6)

This ruler, Nicodemus, visited Lord Jesus when he was crucified, and out of his great devotion to the Lord, brought with him a mixture of myrrh and aloes, which weighed an hundred pounds. Joseph of Arimathaea and Nicodemus, with the help of others, used mixture of myrrh and aloes on the body of Jesus and wrapped the Lord's body in the linen clothing and binding his head with a napkin (cf. John 19:38-40 & 20:7)

And there came also Nicodemus, which at the first came to Jesus by night, and brought a mixture of myrrh and aloes, about an hundred pound weight. (John 19:39)

The Lord's words as to how a matter may be established by the testimony of two or three witnesses was based on the edict that was in Deuteronomy 19:15 and Joseph of Arimathaea, Nicodemus, and Centurion stand as quite good enough witnesses for us to proclaim the truth when someone still has questions about the death, burial and resurrection of Lord Jesus Christ.

But if he will not hear thee, then take with thee one or two more, that in the mouth of two or three witnesses every word may be established. (Matthew 18:16)

One witness shall not rise up against a man for any iniquity, or for any sin, in any sin that he sinneth: at the mouth of two witnesses, or at the mouth of three witnesses, shall the matter be established. (Deuteronomy 19:15)

CENTURION

In addition to two undeniably reliant witnesses of the crucifixion of Jesus, there was another witness, who was a centurion, who standing by the cross watching Jesus die on the cross, thrust his sword into the body of Jesus that went and hit the heart of the Lord. Blood and water gushed forth from the Lord's body as he breathed His last and when there was a great earthquake, the centurion watching these things he loudly proclaimed saying "truly this was the Son of God". The centurion was a Roman soldier, who was a gentile. All those along with the Centurion, who watched the crucifixion and the horrible death of Jesus, acknowledged that Jesus was the "Son of God" (Ref. Matthew 27:54).

SECULAR EVIDENCE

Besides the witnesses recorded in the Bible, there is a record from the Jewish historian, Flavius Joseph who wrote in his "Antiquities of the Jews – Book XVIII Chpater3 Paragraph 3" as follows:

Quote: *Now there was about this time Jesus, a wise man, if it be lawful to call him a man; for he was a doer of wonderful works, a teacher of such men as receive the truth with pleasure. He drew over to him both many of the Jews and many of the Gentiles. He was [the] Christ. And when Pilate, at the suggestion of the principal men amongst us, had condemned him to the cross, (9) those that loved him at the first did not forsake him; for he appeared to them alive again the third day; (10) as the divine prophets had foretold these and ten thousand other wonderful things concerning him. And the tribe of Christians, so named from him, are not extinct at this day. (9) A.D. 33, April 3, (10) April 5.* Unquote

RESURRECTION

The evidence of the resurrection of Lord Jesus Christ is found in Matthew 28:1-20; Mark 16:1-20; Luke 24:1-53, and John 20:1-31 & 21:1-25

Before meditating on the resurrection of Lord Jesus Christ, it is worth recollecting the raising of Lazarus from the dead by Him during His ministry.

Lord Jesus gave instructions to those who were with Martha and Mary to comfort them concerning their brother Lazarus, who was dead for four days. When Jesus said to them to take away the stone, Martha, the sister of Lazarus reluctantly answered and said that his brother was dead for four days and would be stinking by then.

Watching Martha's hesitation, Lord Jesus said to her that if she believed she would see the glory of God. Then, they took away the stone which lay against the grave, where Lazarus was laid. The Lord lifted up His eyes and thanked the Father for hearing His prayer and also affirmed that the Father always hears His prayer.

Jesus spoke these words being confident that the people who were witnessing the miracle would believe in Him and that the Father sent Him. After saying these words Jesus cried with a loud voice saying "Lazarus, come forth".

The dead Lazarus heard the thundering voice of the Lord and he came out of the grave. As was the custom of those days, Lazarus was bound with grave clothes hand and foot before his burial, and he came out with the same clothes and napkin still bound around his face.

Lord Jesus said to them to unloose his bonds, remove his napkin and let him go. As per the instructions of the Lord they did unloose him, removed his napkin from around his face and let him go. (cf. John 11:19-44)

The resurrection of Lazarus, ordered by Lord Jesus Christ was precursor and a glimpse of the resurrection of Lord Jesus Christ. Many Jews, who watched the miracle of Lazarus being raised from the dead, they believed on Him

"Then many of the Jews which came to Mary, and had seen the things which Jesus did, believed on him". (John 11:45)

RESURRECTION OF JESUS

The stone that was laid against the tomb, and which was sealed by the seal of Roman Government was found removed from its place, and the grave was open when Mary Magdalene went to see early in the morning on the first day of the week after the day of Sabbath. From the accounts of other Gospel writers it is understood that there were at least three women along with her.

Gospel writer Mark writes that very early in the morning on the first day of the week Mary Magdalene, and Mary the mother of James, and Salome went to the sepulcher where the body of Jesus was buried. They went there to embalm the body of Jesus in order to keep His body from putrefaction, which confirms that they still did not believe that Jesus would rise from the dead. While they were on their way to the sepulcher they said to themselves as to who would roll away the stone set against the door of the sepulcher.

After their arrival at the sepulcher they found that they stone, which was quite big, was already rolled away. They ventured entering the sepulcher, and on entering they saw a young man in white clothes sitting at the right hand side of the place where Jesus body was supposed to have been there. They were afraid; however the young man consoled them not be afraid and said to them they were seeking Jesus of Nazareth, who was crucified, but He was not there.

The young man pointed to the place where Jesus of Nazareth was laid to rest, and said to them that the Lord rose from the dead and He was not there. He instructed them to go their way and proclaim to the Lord's disciples that the Lord was went ahead of them into Galilee, where they also could see Lord Jesus Christ.

The women quickly left the place because they were afraid. Lord Jesus appeared first to Mary Magdalene, out of whom the Lord had cast away seven devils. His disciples were still mourning and weeping over the death of Jesus and when Mary Magdalene told them about the resurrection of Jesus, they did not believe.

She ran to Simon Peter and to other disciple (John), and said to them in wonder that somebody removed the body of Jesus away from the tomb. She was under the impression that somebody stole the dead body of Jesus.

After the crucifixion, Joseph, the rich counsellor of Arimathaea, who was a disciple of Jesus, went to Pontius Pilate, the governor of the land, and begged him to hand over the body of Jesus to bury in the tomb, which he made for himself.

The tomb was in the garden nearby Golgotha (also called 'Calvary'), where Jesus was crucified. Thus the prophecy in Isaiah 53:9 was fulfilled. He was crucified amid the wicked, bearing our shame and our sin upon Himself, in order that we may be redeemed of our sin, and was buried with the rich.

Pilate granted the request of Joseph of Arimathaea and delivered the dead body of Jesus to be buried in the tomb of Joseph of Arimathaea. After wrapping the Lord's dead body in a clean linen cloth, he was laid in the new tomb, which was hewn out in the rock, and a great stone was rolled closing the door of the sepulcher.

Mary Magdalene, and other Mary, sat over against the sepulcher, till the next day, which was the preparation day. The chief priests and Pharisees went to Pilate and made a petition to him to secure firmly the tomb with a seal, claiming that Jesus had told, while he was alive that he would rise from the dead after three days of His death. Conceding their request Pilate said to them to keep vigil. They sealed the sepulcher very firm and set a watch (cf. Matt. 27:57-66)

Overcoming all these hurdles the Pharisees and Chief priests waited in anticipation of probable failure of Jesus rising from the dead. But, to their dismay and disappointment Lord Jesus Christ was raised by God on the third day. Lord Jesus came out of the grave with glorified body and appeared to many before His ascension after forty days.

During His ministry before crucifixion, Lord Jesus said that the Father loves Him, because He decided to voluntarily lay down His life and taken it again in order to provide a way for sinners to come near Him and accept Him as Savior. No one, by coercion or by force, could take the life of Jesus. He had the power to lay it down and He had the power to take it again. It is because of the voluntary offering of His own body and blood for our sake, the Father loved Him, and it pleased the Father to bruise Jesus, the Son of God, for our sake. He took the form of a servant and came down in the likeness of man to save us (cf. John 10:17-18; Phil. 2:5-11)

Before anyone came near the sepulcher on the first day of the week, there was a great earthquake and the angel of the LORD descended from heaven and rolled back the stone from the door of the sepulcher and sat upon it.

After Peter having received the news from Mary Magdalene, she and Peter ran to the tomb; but the other disciple (John) out ran them and came to the sepulcher. This was on the first day of the week. John stooped into the sepulcher and saw the linen clothes lying in the grave, but he did not enter the sepulcher, perhaps to keep Nazarite vow, or for fear.

However, Peter went into the sepulcher and saw the linen clothes lying aside in the Sepulcher. He observed more importantly, the napkin, with which the face of Jesus was bound, was found lying along with linen clothes, but in a place by itself.

It is interesting to note here that in the case of Lazarus, Lord Jesus ordered removal of linen from the body of Lazarus and unbound him of the napkin that bound his head. In contrast, in the case of Jesus, in the tomb where he was buried, he was not found.

The linen that was used to wrap around his body was lying loose in the sepulcher, and the napkin that bound his face was found lying along with lines, but separately well folded in a place by its place. The linen that was used to bind the dead body of Jesus was lying in the sepulcher.

The napkin that was used to bind the face of dead body of Jesus was found well folded, lying in a place separately by itself along with linen. How is it possible if the concocted stories of Roman Government and others were to be believed that He did not rise again?

Notice the evidences. The seal of the Roman Government was broken. The stone that was against the sepulcher was found removed from its place. The linen that was used to wrap the body of Jesus was found lying in the sepulcher, and the napkin which was used to wrap around the face of the dead body of Jesus was found along with the linen, and yet in a place separately by itself.

From this event and subsequent events, where Lord Jesus appeared physically to many, and other infallible evidences, it is very much clear and worthy of belief that Lord Jesus Christ rose from the dead on the third day of His death on the cross.

The countenance of the angel was like lightning and his clothes were white as snow. The keepers of the tomb fell as dead men, when the saw the brightness of the angel. The women were still surprised to witness these events. The angel of the Lord, then not only proclaimed to the women, of the resurrection of Lord Jesus Christ, but also instructed them to tell others the facts they have seen.

"And the angel answered and said unto the women, Fear not ye: for I know that ye seek Jesus, which was crucified. He is not here: for he is risen, as he said. Come, see the place where the Lord lay. And go quickly, and tell his disciples that he is risen from the dead; and, behold, he goeth before you into Galilee; there shall ye see him: lo, I have told you. And they departed quickly from the sepulchre with fear and great joy; and did run to bring his disciples word". (Matthew 28:5-8)

The women went in obedience to the instructions received from the angel of the Lord and while they were still on their way, Lord Jesus Christ appeared to them, wished them, "All hail". The women saw Him and believed that He is the Christ, and worshipped Him at His feet. Lord Jesus said to them, then they should be afraid, but go and tell His disciples, who had gone into Galilee that they would see the Lord (cf. Matthew 28:1-10)

Interesting to note here is that even after Peter and John believed that Jesus rose again from the dead, Mary was still lingering with the thought that the body of Jesus was stolen. She ardently sought to know where the body was shifted to from its original place of burial. She stood outside the sepulcher weeping, and as she wept, she stooped down into the sepulcher and saw two angels in white sitting, one angel at the head and the other at his feet, where the body of Jesus was laid. The two angels asked Mary as to why she was weeping. She replied saying "they have taken away my Lord, and I know not where they have laid him".

It was at this time that she suddenly turned back and saw that Jesus was standing, and yet she was doubtful if He was Jesus. The Lord spoke to her and asked her why she was weeping and what she was seeking. Mary did not recognize the Lord. She thought he was gardener, and therefore, says to him... "Sir, if thou have borne him hence, tell me where thou hast laid him, and I will take him away".

Mary was so grateful to the Lord that she did not forget the healing Lord Jesus brought about in her. She was there at the tomb look at the dead body of Jesus wherever it was. She was willing to take away the body, if needed.

The devotion of Joseph of Arimathaea, Nicodemus, and Mary need to be pondered on as to how much they honored their Lord and Savior Jesus Christ.

Lord Jesus called her out by her name... "Mary!" It was then that she realized that the one who spoke to her was none other than Lord Jesus Christ Himself. She responded saying "Rabboni", which is to say "Teacher!"

The Lord admonished her not to touch Him, because He has not ascended to His Father, and said to her to tell His brethren, that He will ascend to His Father, who is their Father as well, and thus the Father is God to the Son, and to the disciples as well. It may be recalled that the Father addressed Son as "God" on occasion, thus making it clear that Father and Son are one.

"But unto the Son he saith, Thy throne, O God, is for ever and ever: a sceptre of righteousness is the sceptre of thy kingdom" (Hebrews 1:8)

"Thy throne, O God, is for ever and ever: the sceptre of thy kingdom is a right sceptre. Thou lovest righteousness, and hatest wickedness: therefore God, thy God, hath anointed thee with the oil of gladness above thy fellows" (Psalms 45:6-7)

As per the instructions received from the Lord, Mary Magdalene went to the disciples of Jesus and proclaimed the resurrection of the Lord and witnessed to them that she saw the Lord, personally. The disciples assembled on the same day, which was the first day of the week, the resurrection day of Lord Jesus Christ. They assembled in a house for the fear of Jews.

However, they saw the Lord coming into the house even when the doors of the house were yet closed. That was the glorious body Lord Jesus had after His resurrection. He could pass through the closed doors into the house and comfort His disciples. He came into the house and stood in the midst of them, and said to them "Peace be unto you".

Lest they should still remain in unbelief, the Lord Jesus showed unto them his hands that were nailed, and his side that was pierced. The disciples were exceedingly glad when the saw Lord Jesus Christ. Jesus said to them once again, "Peace be unto you" and declared that as the Father had sent Him, even so, the

Lord was sending them into the world to proclaim the good news about the Father, the Son and the Holy Spirit.

Lord Jesus Christ consoled them and after wishing peace on them, he breathed on them…"and said, "Receive the Holy Spirit. If you forgive anyone's sins, their sins are forgiven; if you do not forgive them, they are not forgiven." John 20:21-23

The power given by Lord Jesus Christ to His disciples was equal in all aspects. None of the disciples, even Peter did not get some extra blessings in terms of the power that the Lord gave to them. He said to all His disciples, "whosoever sins ye remit; they are remitted unto them…"

Notwithstanding of the breathing of Holy Spirit on them, and the power the Lord gave them, yet the commission to proclaim the Gospel of Jesus Christ was to be done only after the Pentecost was fully come. The festival "Pentecost" was to come on the fiftieth day after resurrection of Jesus Christ. After His resurrection, the Lord remained on this earth for forty days and appeared to many. After forty days are completed the Lord ascended into heaven. His disciples were asked to wait for the gift of Holy Spirit to descend upon them. As instructed by the Lord, they waited in upper room in Jerusalem, until fiftieth day, when Holy Spirit came upon them and they spoke to tongues, understanding everyone's language by the other. Thus they all glorified God.

When Lord Jesus Christ appeared to His disciples in a closed room, and wished them "peace be unto you", standing in their midst, and followed by bestowal upon them of the power of Holy Spirit to remit sins of whosoever they wish to remit, and retain the sins of those, whose sins they wish to retain, Thomas, one of His disciples, who was also called Didymus, was not present among them. On receiving the information from his colleagues that they all saw risen Lord Jesus Christ, Thomas did not believe and said to them that unless he places his hands in the nail marks of Lord Jesus Christ, and thrust his hand into the pierced side of the Lord, he would not believe in the resurrection of Jesus.

Lord Jesus did not neglect the unbelieving disciple, but took care of Him to thwart away his unbelief and make him great again. On another occasion, when all the disciples were together, and the doors of the house were shut, Thomas also was with them. It was just eight days from the previous incident.

The Lord then, appeared to all the disciples and standing in their midst in the room where they gathered, and wished them saying "Peace be unto you".

Then, the Lorde said to Thomas... "Reach hither thy finger, and behold my hands; and reach hither thy hand, and thrust it into my side: and be not faithless, but believing. And Thomas answered and said unto him, My Lord and my God. Jesus saith unto him". Thomas saw the Lord and saw the nail marks in the hands of Lord Jesus, and he also saw the side of Jesus where there the soldier had pierced with the sword, and called out loudly, "My Lord and my God".

Lord Jesus admonished Thomas saying blessed are those who have not seen, and yet believed in the death, burial and resurrection of the Lord, unlike Thomas, who preferred to believe in the resurrection of Jesus, only after physically testing the Lord.

After this incident the Lord did many other signs in the presence of His disciples, and John did not record all of them in the "the Book of John". Sufficient were the details he mentioned in the Gospel according to him for people to believe that Jesus is the Christ, the Son of God, and by believing in Him they might have life through His name (cf. John 20:1-31)

THE TWO SAW JESUS AT EMMAUS

The names of the two men who saw Jesus, but did not recognize Him, were Cleopas, and Peter. (Some believe the second one was Luke). They were walking down the road at Emmaus talking interesting news of the day. Jesus had promised that He would rise from the dead on the third day after His crucifixion, and it was the third day when the two were walking down the road at Emmaus on their way to Jerusalem. They were deeply discussing about the crucifixion, burial and resurrection of Jesus Christ.

To their surprise a third one joined them on their way to Jerusalem, and inquired as to what they were discussing about. They saw Jesus but did not recognize Him. Was it accidental that they did not recognize Jesus? No, it was according to the plan of God. Read...

"And it came to pass, that, while they communed together and reasoned, Jesus himself drew near, and went with them. But

their eyes were holden that they should not know him" (Luke 24:15-16)

Cleopas answered by questioning the Lord if He did not know the important events and burning issues of the season in that area. Of course, Jesus knew of every detail, yet He questioned them in order to inquire deep into their knowledge of the events, and to get their clear view before He disclosed Himself. Cleopas, then answered Jesus that he was talking about Jesus of Nazareth.

Cleopas went on explaining that Jesus was to restore to them the kingdom of Israel which was divided. However, the chief priests and the rulers delivered Jesus to be crucified. He also explained that certain women went to the tomb that morning and did not find the body of Jesus in the sepulcher.

Indeed, Jesus had said earlier that Father loves Him because He promised to lay down His life and would take it back again. He had said that no one had the power to take life from Him but He has the absolute power to lay down His life and take it back again. It pleased the Father to bruise Him on the cross for our sake because the ultimate purpose was to see that we are saved and receive everlasting life.

After hearing explanation from Cleopas, Lord Jesus said unto them...

"...O fools, and slow of heart to believe all that the prophets have spoken: Ought not Christ to have suffered these things, and to enter into his glory? And beginning at Moses and all the prophets, he expounded unto them in all the scriptures the things concerning himself" (Luke 24:25-27)

Lord Jesus Christ was referring to the Old Testament Scriptures about Him and they are...Genesis 3:15; 49:10; Numbers 21:8-9; Deuteronomy 18:15; Isaiah 9:6-7; 53:1-12; Psalm 16:1-11,1-11,1-7; Daniel 9:25-27; Malachi 4:2-6.

As they were nearing the village, the Lord was walking further away from them, when they made a plea to Him to stay with them for the night because it was getting dark. The Lord agreed to stay with them. As they all sat eat their supper, the Lord took bread and blessed it, and broke it, and gave to them. It was then that their eyes were open and they understood that He was none other than Jesus Himself. However, the Lord disappeared from their sight and went away.

They recollected the Lord's talk with them, opening up scriptures before them, as they walked toward the village, and marveled. Without wasting any more time they got up and walked to Jerusalem. There they saw the eleven disciples (the ten and Mathias; Judas Iscariot having been dead by then), and others with them and said to them "The Lord is risen indeed", and has appeared to Simon Peter. They also explained to them as to how they saw Jesus, and yet did not recognize Him, at first sight, on their way to Emmaus, but that their eyes were opened when the Lord broke bread and blessed and gave it to them. They recognized Lord Jesus Christ only after they ate the bread the Lord broke for them after blessing it. (cf. Luke 24:13-35)

CHAPTER 20

LOVE IS GREATER THAN SPIRITUAL GIFTS

The three chapters from 1 Corinthians in the New Testament are written by Apostle Paul by the inspiration of God. These three chapters form a set of one theme dealing with love which is greater than the spiritual gifts.

Paul's focus in these three chapters, from 12 to 14, is love, a divine love, which is "Agape love".

All other points discussed in these chapters are subservient to the main theme, which is "Love". It becomes hard to understand when greater focus is laid upon spiritual gifts sidelining the "love" aspect. There is no point in emphasizing on any of the Spiritual gifts mentioned in these three chapters without focusing on 'love'.

None of the spiritual gifts take greater importance than the divine love one should have towards another. The moment one neglects to lay emphasis on divine love and discuss the details of the Spiritual gifts controversies as to which spiritual gift is greater than the other, and whether those spiritual gifts are in existence now or not, take precedence in debates.

The first and foremost fact is to acknowledge that "Jesus is Lord". No one, who is led by the Holy Spirit would deny that Jesus is Lord, nor would say "Jesus is accursed".

CHAPTER 21

WHAT IS SPIRITUAL GIFT?

Spiritual Gift is God's special empowerment of every believer in Christ by the Holy Spirit in order to fulfill the ministry of the Lord Jesus Christ and to add souls to the kingdom of God. The Spiritual gifts are given by His grace for the use within the Body of Christ.

All these Spiritual gifts are given by one and the same Spirit. Holy Spirit apportions to each believer individually as He desires and according to His will that the name of Lord Jesus Christ may be glorified and souls may be added to the kingdom of God.

There are variety of Spiritual gifts, but every one of them is from the one and only one Holy Spirit. The Lord is one and only one for us, and everyone, who is born again, would do some kind of service to the Lord to please Him. All humanity is the creation of God, and all do not accept that Jesus is Lord. Bible is clear about the fact that Salvation is of the Lord and it is by none other than Lord Jesus Christ. He is the Savior. He is our only mediator, and high priest. All power is given to Him and to Him alone.

The Lord demands love from us because He is love, and He first loved us. Not that we loved God first, but God loved us first, and He sent His one only Son into this world that He may bear our sins and die on behalf of us, and rise from the dead on the third day. Just as He was raised from the dead, all those who are born again will be raised from the dead with glorified bodies to meet the Lord in the mid-air, when He comes again. Everyone to whom the status as the 'child of God' is assigned will be conformed to His image and will be with Him forever and ever.

God expects from us to love not only Him, but also every human being, just as He loved. This love is greater than any spiritual gift any one may have. All the spiritual gifts which are given to the born-again children of God will vanish away one day or the other, and what remains is only the divine love. We see everything in partial knowledge now, but we will acquire full knowledge when we see the Lord face to face. Until then we will have partial knowledge, partial gifts of Spiritual gifts. None of the Spiritual gifts enlisted in the Bible are of any use when we see the Lord face to face. Every spiritual gift is given to the born again children of God in different measures as the Lord pleases, and every spiritual gift is given for the purpose of edification of either self or church. However, the ultimate goal is to praise the Lord.

CHAPTER 22

THE THREE VERSES

There are in 1 Corinthians 12th Chapter three verses which are very important with regard understanding what the Spiritual gifts are and why they are given to believers.

"Now there are varieties of gifts, but the same Spirit" 1 Corinthians 12:4 (ESV)
"and there are varieties of service, but the same Lord" 1 Corinthians 12:5 (ESV)
" and there are varieties of activities, but it is the same God who empowers them all in everyone" 1 Corinthians 12:6 (ESV)

Verse 4 states here are varieties of gifts but the same Spirit
Verse 5 states that there are varieties of service but the same Lord
Verse 6 states that there are varieties of activities, but the same God

Interestingly, the Trinity (Spirit, the Lord, and God) can be seen in these verses. Also it is clear that the gifts are various, services are various, and activities are various, but all of them are from the Same Spirit, Same Lord, and Same God, who works in all believers.

The purpose of all the gifts or manifestations are for the expansion of the kingdom of God. As we read further there are many members in the body of Christ, but all of them with various gifts, work for the Lord and to bring glory to God.

The various types of ministries or services for God are mentioned in 1 Corinthians 12:5 are seen in 1 Corinthians 12:27-28, and in Ephesians 4:11-12 and also in Romans 12:4-10

"Now ye are the body of Christ, and members in particular. And God hath set some in the church, first apostles, secondarily prophets, thirdly teachers, after that miracles, then gifts of healings, helps, governments, diversities of tongues". (1 Corinthians 12:27-28)

"And he gave some, apostles; and some, prophets; and some, evangelists; and some, pastors and teachers; for the perfecting of the saints, for the work of the ministry, for the edifying of the body of Christ" (Ephesians 4:11-12)

"For as in one body we have many members, and the members do not all have the same function so we, though many, are one body in Christ, and individually members one of another. Having gifts that differ according to the grace given to us, let us use them: if prophecy, pin proportion to our faith; if service, in our serving; the one who teaches, in his teaching; the one who exhorts, in his exhortation; the one who contributes, in generosity; the one who leads, with zeal; the one who does acts of mercy, with cheerfulness" Romans 12:4-8 (ESV)

There is also admonition for the believers that our love for one another should be genuine, with brotherly affection, outdoing one another in showing honor; and also that should abhor that which is evil, and hold fast to what is good. This admonition helps great deal to avoid skirmishes among believers as to which gift or manifestation is greater than the other. As we see in the real world, many believers condemn fellow believers for non-possession of gifts, or manifestations that they do possess. The Scriptures are clear that all the gifts and manifestations are equal in the sight of the Lord and every gift or manifestation is given for bringing glory to God.

"Let love be genuine. Abhor what is evil; hold fast to what is good. Love one another with brotherly affection. Outdo one another in showing honor" Romans 12:9-10 (ESV).

Verse 6 indicates the activities or operations of the Spiritual things of the Holy Spirit.

But the manifestation of the Spirit is given to every man to profit withal. (1 Corinthians 12:7)

Every Spiritual gift is given for the manifestation of the Spirit for the common good.

1. The utterance of wisdom
2. The utterance of knowledge
3. Faith
4. Gifts of healing
5. The working of miracles
6. Prophecy
7. Ability to distinguish between spirits
8. Various kinds of tongues,
9. The interpretation of tongues.

"But the manifestation of the Spirit is given to every man to profit withal. For to one is given by the Spirit the word of wisdom; to another the word of knowledge by the same Spirit; To another faith by the same Spirit; to another the gifts of healing by the same Spirit; to another the working of miracles; to another prophecy; to another discerning of spirits; to another

divers kinds of tongues; to another the interpretation of tongues: But all these worketh that one and the selfsame Spirit, dividing to every man severally as he will" (1 Corinthians 12:7-11)

All these Spiritual gifts are given by one and the same Spirit. Holy Spirit apportions to each believer individually as He desires and according to His will that the name of Lord Jesus Christ may be glorified and souls may be added to the kingdom of God.

The ultimate purpose is to add souls to the Kingdom of God. These gifts not for becoming wealthy by exercising these gifts, nor to show off one's power over another. These gifts are not purchasable, but freely given by God to those who seek for them.

Not everyone can have all the gifts, but God gives to one a gift or two or more according to His desire and purpose. Simon the sorcerer tried to buy the gifts of the Holy Spirit but Peter chased him out.

"And when Simon saw that through laying on of the apostles' hands the Holy Ghost was given, he offered them money, Saying, Give me also this power, that on whomsoever I lay hands, he may receive the Holy Ghost. But Peter said unto him, Thy money perish with thee, because thou hast thought that the gift of God may be purchased with money" (Acts 8:18-20)

CHAPTER 23

ONE BODY WITH MANY MEMBERS

Paul compares the Church and its members with the body of a man. A body has head and several members. Though the members of the body have different functions, the body is one, and they serve one purpose. The head controls every member of the body; so is Lord Jesus Christ. The head of the Church is Lord Jesus Christ.

The members of the body, though be many, are one body. All the born-again children of God are equal members of the Church and are baptized into one body, whether they be Jews, or Gentiles, or slaves or free. They all are made to drink from the same Spirit.

The foot cannot say to the hand that it does not belong to the body because it is not hand, nor would ear could say to eye that it does not belong to the body because it is not eye. Every member of the body is equally important and every part is needed for the well-functioning of the body.

Imagine if whole body were to be an eye, or hand, where would the sense of hearing be and how the body would walk. Not a single part of the body is inferior to the other every member of the body is important in its place and in its function.

Neither eye could say to the hand that it has no need of the hand in the body, nor could head say to the feet that they are not needed in the body. Also, not a single part can voluntarily say that it does not belong to the body nor is there any use of it in the body. They all serve one purpose; the existence of a complete structure with head and the body with many equal members to ultimately bring glory to the head. Important point to be recognized here is that if there is no head, the body has no recognition, and the body cannot exist on its own.

There are some parts in the body that seem to be weaker and less honorable, but God made them to be indispensable. They are unpresentable but are treated with greater modesty than those parts that are presentable.

God so composed the body that He gave greater honor to the parts that lacked it, in order that there may not be division in the body. God desires that all members of the body may have same care for one another. If one member of the body suffers, every other member of the body suffers as well and so is every member rejoices if one member is honored.

CHAPTER 24

SHOULD WE WAIT FOR HOLY SPIRIT

"And I will pray the Father, and he shall give you another Comforter, that he may abide with you for ever; Even the Spirit of truth; whom the world cannot receive, because it seeth him not, neither knoweth him: but ye know him; for he dwelleth with you, and shall be in you" (John 14:16-17)"I will not leave you comfortless: I will come to you". (John 14:18)

"But the Comforter, which is the Holy Ghost, whom the Father will send in my name, he shall teach you all things, and bring all things to your remembrance, whatsoever I have said unto you. Peace I leave with you, my peace I give unto you: not as the world giveth, give I unto you. Let not your heart be troubled, neither let it be afraid" (John 14:26-27)

• The last portion of John 14:17 says "He dwelleth with you, and shall be in you". That is, Holy Spirit was with us when we are born-again, and He is in us from the time when we are born-again. Notice the words of Lord Jesus. He said...

• "Jesus saith unto him, I am the way, the truth, and the life: no man cometh unto the Father, but by me". (John 14:6) "… no one cometh unto the Father, but by me".

• The Lord will not leave us comfortless.

• The Comforter, who is the Holy Spirit, whom the Father sent in Jesus' name, is teaching us and will teach us all things.

WHY THEN PAUL ASKED FEW MEN IN EPHESUS?

"And it came to pass, that, while Apollos was at Corinth, Paul having passed through the upper coasts came to Ephesus: and finding certain disciples, He said unto them, Have ye received the Holy Ghost since ye believed? And they said unto him, We have not so much as heard whether there be any Holy Ghost. And he said unto them, Unto what then were ye baptized? And they said, Unto John's baptism. Then said Paul, John verily baptized with the baptism of repentance, saying unto the people, that they should believe on him which should come after him, that is, on Christ Jesus. When they heard this, they were baptized in the name of the Lord Jesus. And when Paul had laid his hands upon them, the Holy Ghost came on them; and they spake with tongues, and prophesied. And all the men were about twelve". (Acts 19:1-7)

• Have you received Holy Spirit since you believed?

What was Paul asking and what answer they gave? From their answer it is very much evident that they were not believers in Jesus Christ. If they were believers in Christ, they would have been led by Holy Spirit and in them would Holy Spirit lived, and they would have known about that fact. They said they were baptized unto John's baptism. But John Himself said the one (Jesus) who comes after him is greater than Himself. John's baptism was not of faith in Jesus Christ but of repentance. Obviously they were not of Jesus Christ, but of John.

Romans 8:9, and 1 Corinthians 6:19 show that if a person does not have the Holy Spirit, then he does not belong to Christ.

It is when they said that they were baptized unto John, Paul said to them that they should believe on Jesus Christ. When they heard this fact, they were baptized in the name of Lord Jesus. When Paul laid hands on them, Holy Spirit came on them, and they spoke tongues, which are languages understood by everyone as we read in Acts 2:9-11. They all gathered on the occasion of Passover festival on the day of Pentecost, which is 50th day after resurrection of Lord Jesus Christ.

Parthians, and Medes, and Elamites, and the dwellers in Mesopotamia, and in Judaea, and Cappadocia, in Pontus, and Asia, Phrygia, and Pamphylia, in Egypt, and in the parts of Libya about Cyrene, and strangers of Rome, Jews and proselytes, Cretes and Arabians, who spoke different languages, understood the languages of one another. (Ref. Acts 2:9-11)

"And even things without life giving sound, whether pipe or harp, except they give a distinction in the sounds, how shall it be known what is piped or harped? For if the trumpet give an uncertain sound, who shall prepare himself to the battle? So likewise ye, except ye utter by the tongue words easy to be understood, how shall it be known what is spoken? for ye shall speak into the air" (1 Corinthians 14:7-9)

CHAPTER 25

LIVING SACRIFICE

"I beseech you therefore, brethren, by the mercies of God, that ye present your bodies a living sacrifice, holy, acceptable unto God, which is your reasonable service" (Romans 12:1)

Apostle Paul uses a unique word, 'beseech' while addressing Chief Captain (Acts 21:39), King Agrippa (Acts 26:3), brethren at Rome (Romans 12:1 and 15:30) brethren at Corinthians (1 Cor.1:10), which shows how loving and humble he was in his approach with others. 'Beseech' means to beg anxiously, or to request earnestly.

In this verse Paul requests earnestly his fellow believers at Rome to present their bodies a living sacrifice. What exactly 'living sacrifice' means? In the Old Testament period, the physical sacrifices are made to God to have reconciliation with him by way of 'Atonement' for the sin man had committed. The sacrifices could be a goat, a lamb, or turtledoves.

Inasmuch as Christ became our 'propitiation', we in this New Testament period are no longer required to offer the physical offerings. Christ's blood that was shed and His body that bore our sins is enough for salvation. All that an unbeliever has to do is to believe this fact, confess his/her sins to Lord Jesus, and accept him as "Lord" and believe in heart that God raised Him from the dead. After that we continually offer our bodies as living sacrifice unto God.

The believers in Christ are to show kindness, humbleness of mind, meekness, and longsuffering (Col. 3:12), present bodies as holy temple because the Spirit of God lives in us (1 Corinthians 3:16), and worship him in truth and sprit. This is the reasonable service unto him. The true worship is not a forced one, but of voluntary and emanates from the bottom of heart, offering ourselves fully unto him with complete devotion.

"Know ye not that ye are the temple of God, and that the Spirit of God dwelleth in you?" (1 Corinthians 3:16)

CHAPTER 26

APOSTLE PAUL'S TESTIMONY

"Rejoice greatly, O daughter of Zion! Shout aloud, O daughter of Jerusalem! Behold, your king is coming to you; righteous and having salvation is he, humble and mounted on a donkey, on a colt, the foal of a donkey" (Zechariah 9:9 ESV)

"Say to the daughter of Zion, 'Behold, your king is coming to you, humble, and mounted on a donkey, on a colt, the foal of a beast of burden.'" (Matthew 21:5 ESV)

Paul, in his testimony before King Agrippa said that before his conversion to Christianity he had much grudge and hatred toward Christians and their beliefs. Therefore, he decided to do many things contrary to the name of Lord Jesus Christ of Nazareth. He had shut up many Christians in prisons with the authority that he received from the chief priests and voiced against them when they were put to death. He punished believers in synagogue and compelled them to blaspheme Christ. His hatred towards Christians was so great that he persecuted them in even in unknown cities. Moreover, he obtained letter of authority from chief priest and was going to Damascus to execute his purpose.

Paul's addressing excels anybody's expectations that even in such a great disadvantageous position as prisoner as he was, he exclaims with much emotion "At midday, O king" and then proceeds. The way he addresses is so pleasing"

"At midday, O king, I saw in the way a light from heaven, above the brightness of the sun, shining round about me and them which journeyed with me" (Acts 26:13)

Paul's addressing next is again so pleasing

"Whereupon, O king Agrippa, I was not disobedient unto the heavenly vision" (Acts 26:19)

Paul was speaking about his conversion. He narrates as to how a great light from heaven shone around midday and Paul and all those who accompanied him fell down to the ground.

Only Paul heard a voice in Hebrew tongue from heaven that questioned him "Saul,. Saul why persecutest me? It is hard for you to kick against pricks" Then Paul cried out saying "Who art thou Lord?" and the voice said "I am Jesus whom thou persecutest". But the voice from Lord Jesus Christ comforted Paul.

The Lord said to Ananias that Paul was a chosen vessel to minister the word of God and be a witness for Him, of all that he has seen, and that which he would see in future. Lord Jesus Christ sent Paul specifically to carry His Gospel to the Gentiles.

Paul said to King Agrippa that he was not disobedient to the vision and command that he received from heaven. He preached Gospel of Jesus Christ at Damascus, at Jerusalem, at Judea and Samaria and then in uttermost parts of the earth to the Gentiles. The message he carried was that those who hear the Gospel of Jesus Christ should repent of their sins to Lord Jesus Christ and receive salvation.

It was this reason why Paul was caught by Jews in the temple and they made attempts to kill him. As he obtained command and help from God he continued preaching none other beliefs than that the prophets and Moses spoke of. He spoke of prophecies that were fulfilled in Lord Jesus Christ. He preached that Christ who was spoken of by prophets needs to have come, die for the sins of mankind and be the first among the resurrected. He preached that Christ suffered death and showed light unto the Gentiles as also to the Jews.

Paul indeed realized that it is hard to kick against the pricks!

===================

CHAPTER 27

OUR SAVIOR

In the beginning God created the heaven and the earth. And the earth was without form, and void; and darkness was upon the face of the deep. And the Spirit of God moved upon the face of the waters. And God said, Let there be light: and there was light. And God saw the light, that it was good: and God divided the light from the darkness. And God called the light Day, and the darkness he called Night. And the evening and the morning were the first day". (Genesis 1:1-5)

"In the beginning was the Word, and the Word was with God, and the Word was God. The same was in the beginning with God" (John 1:1-2)

From John 1:1-2 we understand that our Lord Jesus Christ is the creator. God is Triune: the Father the Son, and the Holy Spirit. They are co-equal, co-existent but their functions are different, and yet they are all One; and God is One. This is mystery and it is very hard to understand!

"And the Word was made flesh, and dwelt among us, (and we beheld his glory, the glory as of the only begotten of the Father,) full of grace and truth". (John 1:14)

What a great statement it is that the Word became flesh and dwelt among us. The Word became a living being and lived among us. The Word was none other than Lord Jesus Christ and in Him we have redemption through his blood, even the forgiveness of sins.

We have redemption from the bondage of sin in none but Lord Jesus Christ, who is the image of the invisible God. He is the first born of every creature and by Him were all the things created that are in heaven, and in earth visible and invisible, whether they be thrones, or dominions, or principalities, or powers.

Lord Jesus Christ is the creator and He created everything for Him. He was before all things and by Him all things consist. He is the head of the Church and He is the beginning and the firstborn from the dead. He is Alpha and Omega. He has the keys of hell and death. (Cf. Colossians 1:14-20 and Revelation 1)

"In whom we have redemption through his blood, even the forgiveness of sins: Who is the image of the invisible God, the firstborn of every creature: For by him were all things created, that are in heaven, and that are in earth, visible and invisible, whether they be thrones, or dominions, or principalities, or powers: all things were created by him, and for him: And he is before all things, and by him all things consist. And he is the head of the body, the church: who is the beginning, the firstborn from the dead; that in all things he might have the preeminence. For it pleased the Father that in him should all fulness dwell; And, having made peace through the blood of his cross, by him to reconcile all things unto himself; by him, I say, whether they be things in earth, or things in heaven" (Colossians 1:14-20 and Revelation 22:13)

The writer of Hebrews describes in the book of Hebrews Chapter 1 that the Father has appointed His Son, Lord Jesus

Christ, the heir of all things and by whom also He made all the worlds. Jesus was the brightness of the glory of the Father, and express image of His person, upholding all things by the word of His power.

It pleased the Father to bruise the Son for our sake in order to redeem us from the bondage of sin. Lord Jesus Christ purged our sins and sat down on the right hand of the Majesty on high. Jesus did not die as martyr, or good man, or innocent man, but He voluntarily became sacrifice on behalf us, paid penalty on behalf us in order to redeem us. (Cf. Hebrews 1:1-10 and John Ch.19)

The blood of Jesus, the Son of God cleanses us from all sin, and the entire hope of redemption that we have, the entire hope of eternity, lies in the fact that Jesus got the job done on the cross. Think of Jesus yielding to the shouts of those men who were witnesses at the cross of Calvary that if He was the Son of God He should come down, save Him and save others. If only Jesus yielded to their shouts and gotten down from the cross before He died, He would not have completed the task he took upon Him to accomplish.

When Jesus said, "It is finished he said, "It is finished" because He had accomplished all that He had to accomplish and it was finished. Nothing more needs to be added to our redemption, or nothing more can be added to our redemption. Jesus finished the task and it ended there. It does not need someone else go after Him to complete any task that might anyone think is left behind; no nothing is left behind, and no one needs to do anything more.

The task of creation was in the hands of Jesus and He finished it. The task of redemption was in the hands of Jesus and He finished it. It was at the cross when He is about to die, He said, "It is finished" because nothing more needed to be accomplished for our redemption from sin that He died on the cross and rose from the dead on the third day with incorruptible body. We cannot add our good works to the finished work of salvation by Lord Jesus Christ.

===========================

CHAPTER 28

PEACE AND SAFETY FOR HIS CHILDREN

I will both lay me down in peace, and sleep: for thou, LORD, only makest me dwell in safety. (Psalms 4:8)

"I will both lay me down in peace, and sleep: for thou, LORD, only makest me dwell in safety" Psalm 4:8

King David's life is filled with experiences worth noting, and they are very useful for our exhortation, glorying God in our lives, and for reproof, where necessary. Although he committed serious sins in his life, yet because he confessed his sins to God, he was forgiven, and God called him a man after His own heart not because God approved David's sin, but because he pursued God's ways.

King Saul pursued after his own heart, while David went after the heart of God. Even though God rejected Saul, he did not reject His own people, Israel. And, David was the right choice to be the king over Israel, according to God. The LORD raised a king over Israel, a man whose heart was as compassionate as His, was. God loved Israel and the children of Israel.

"And when he had removed him, he raised up unto them David to be their king; to whom also he gave testimony, and said, I have found David the [son] of Jesse, a man after mine own heart, which shall fulfil all my will" Acts 13:22

David's turmoil, troubles, loss of peace of mind on certain occasions, trials were all within the permissive limits of God.

Some of the facts of his life are, as God said, the sword shall never depart from his house; he shall not build a house for the Lord, but his desire shall be fulfilled by his son, Solomon.

The occasion when Psalm 4 was written by David is not revealed in the Scriptures. However, David's acknowledgment of God's help in times of need, and his cry over his enemies and his comfort in the LORD, are clearly evident. His prayer was so passionate and intense that God could not have gone without answering him.

As for us, the New Testament believers, we have the "New Covenant" made by Lord Jesus Christ, who wrote the laws into our hearts, and in our minds. It has to do with the inner transformation, and complete forgiveness. Unlike the requirements of offering sacrifices, time and again, we have our sins forgiven once and for all, and God does not remember them anymore. This promise is not only for the children of Israel, but in Christ Jesus, it is for every believer in Christ, whose sins are forgiven. Throw away that negative interpretation that is applicable only to the children of Israel.

"This is the covenant that I will make with them after those days, saith the Lord, I will put my laws into their hearts, and in their minds will I write them; And their sins and iniquities will I remember no more" (Hebrews 10:16-17)

"And to Jesus the mediator of the new covenant, and to the blood of sprinkling, that speaketh better things than that of Abel" (Hebrews 12:24)

David was ruler of Israel according to the choice God made, and today God is calling those, who follow His desires to enlighten the world with the truth of the knowledge of the living God. Answer His call. He needs people whose hearts follow His desires, rather than their own.

David addresses God, in Psalm 4:1, as God of righteousness, thus acknowledging God's love and mercy towards him. He gave pre-eminence to God in his prayer, and depended on Him, before he ventured on any serious task.

David acknowledged that God enlarged him when he was in distress. He sought God's mercy upon him. His acknowledgment of God's help recalls his victory over philistine giant, Goliath, and in many battles. He was known as 'man of wars', and rightly so, he was triumphant in all, but one battle, where he counted the number of men his army. God said to him to rely fully on Him, but on one occasion, he counted his own strength, and when he tried to depend on his own strength he failed.

When we depend on God we are sure of gaining victory because God is mighty; but when we depend on our strength, we often face defeats, because our strength is limited, and may not be as mighty as of the enemy is. Therefore, it is essential that we always seek God's help, and depend on His strength, because His strength never fails. He delivered the children of Israel with His mighty and outstretched arm; and He is available for us too, for delivering us from our stressful, disastrous and trying situations.

David saw in his life, people, who turned his glory into shame, and, therefore, he questioned them as to how long they would try to bring shame to him. He questioned them if they wished to continue to love vanity. He wanted them to know that the LORD has set apart His people, for Himself, and says that he being one such man, who was set apart for God, the LORD will hear them when he calls unto Him in prayer.

Therefore, David admonishes those who try to bring shame to him, to stand in awe of God and not sin; but introspect themselves when they are on their beds, and be calm. He advises them to offer sacrifices of righteousness, and trust in the LORD.

Many would say to him as to who would do any good to them, but David trusts in the LORD and seeks His help on behalf all of them. He acknowledges that God has put gladness in his heart, more when he was in distress, rather than in situations of abundance, and plenteous of material possessions.

Then, he consoles himself and lays down to sleep in peace because he was sure that he will abide in the LORD's safety.

People, during the time when Lord Jesus Christ was on this earth, tried to bring shame to His glorious works, yet He bore our sins on Him. He died for our sake on the cross bearing our sin to redeem us from our sin. He was buried, and was raised on the third day. Whosoever believes that He is the Lord and believes in his heart that God raised Him from the dead will receive everlasting life. (cf... 2 Corinthians 5:21, Romans 10:9, John 3:16) It is only by grace through faith in Him that saves us from perishing

CHAPTER 29 LIVNG STONES

In order for born-again children to be living stones in the spiritual building that is being built for the LORD, the Holy Bible says all evil traits should be laid aside. Peter, the disciple of Jesus Christ, lists in 1 Peter 2:1 these evil attributes as...

1. Malice
2. Deceit
3. Hypocrisy
4. Envy, and
5. All evil speaking

MALICE:

Malice It is a desire on the part of a person to do harm or to commit intentional wrongful act on others. Leaven symbolizes sin. Apostle Paul writes to Corinthians in his first epistle that just as Jews fully removed leaven from the Passover feast, we in the New Testament period should remove all malice and evil from within us. James, the half-brother of Jesus writes that we should lay apart all filthiness and receive the word of God. The Word alone saves our souls. Malice is inflammation of angry heart that devises ruin of another person and eventually making merry in it.

"Let us therefore celebrate the festival, not with the old leaven, the leaven of malice and evil, but with the unleavened bread of sincerity and truth" 1 Cor. 5:8

"Wherefore lay apart all filthiness and superfluity of naughtiness, and receive with meekness the engrafted word, which is able to save your souls" (James 1:21)

DECEIT:

Deceit is the distortion of truth by flattery, or by misleading, or by causing delusion. It is achieved by imposing falsehood craftily on others, taking undue advantage of their weakness or ignorance. Bible condemns deceit and warns to be careful not be deceived.

"No one who practices deceit shall dwell in my house; no one who utters lies shall continue before my eyes." (Psalms 101:7)

"See to it that no one takes you captive by philosophy and empty deceit, according to human tradition, according to the elemental spirits of the world, and not according to Christ"
Colossians 2:8

HYPOCRISY

Hypocrisy is to pretend as having a virtuous character, which one does not really have, and to pretend of being a true friend, which in reality one is not. In religious circles hypocrisy is to show false piety, and to pretend of having moral and religious beliefs, which one does not truly possess.

Lord Jesus Christ condemned hypocrisy of Pharisees in Matthew 23:1-39

"But all their works they do for to be seen of men: they make broad their phylacteries, and enlarge the borders of their garments, and love the uppermost rooms at feasts, and the chief seats in the synagogues, and greetings in the markets, and to be called of men, Rabbi, Rabbi" (Matthew 23:5-7)

ENVY

Envy is feeling jealous of others success, advantages, and possessions, and desire to acquire wealth by wrongful acts. Greediness to acquire money, power and having lustful eyes on other gender are the main causes of contentions, fights and wars in this world. This is one of the sins a man easily falls into. Bible condemns envy and provides answer not to be envious.

"For where envying and strife is, there is confusion and every evil work" (James 3:16)

"Ye lust, and have not: ye kill, and desire to have, and cannot obtain: ye fight and war, yet ye have not, because ye ask not. Ye ask, and receive not, because ye ask amiss, that ye may consume it upon your lusts" (James 4:2-3)

"There hath no temptation taken you but such as is common to man: but God is faithful, who will not suffer you to be tempted above that ye are able; but will with the temptation also make a way to escape, that ye may be able to bear it" (1 Corinthians 10:13)

EVIL SPEAKING

Evil speaking is defaming others, usually called as 'backbiting'. It is "slander". Bible condemns evil speaking.

"Do not speak evil against one another, brothers. The one who speaks against a brother or judges his brother, speaks evil against the law and judges the law. But if you judge the law, you are not a doer of the law but a judge" James 4:11

Bible cautions Christians to be careful of not falling into these sins, namely, "malice", "deceit", "hypocrisy", "envy", and "evil speaking". Even though one is born again, one is likely to come across many situations, where one would deliberately or inadvertently fall into these sins. God is gracious and longsuffering to forgive if one repents sincerely. It is then that a Christian becomes a living stone to occupy a place in the building the Lord is building.

We, as living stones, should be pure and sanctified to be used by the Lord, in building a spiritual house for Himself. We are a holy and royal priesthood, and are required to offer up not animal sacrifices, or human sacrifices, but spiritual sacrifices acceptable unto God through our only mediator Lord Jesus Christ.

The covenants and blessings belonged to Israel; however, by the mercy of God and through Lord Jesus Christ, gentiles have been given the privilege of being partakers of the promises of God.

"That the Gentiles should be fellow-heirs, and of the same body, and partakers of his promise in Christ by the gospel" (Ephesians 3:6)

"Having abolished in his flesh the enmity, even the law of commandments contained in ordinances; for to make in himself of twain one new man, so making peace" (Ephesians 2:15)

Holy Bible instructs us to abstain from fleshly lusts that war against our soul, and to conduct to be honorable among the people of this world. The word of God does not encourage avenging offenders, but rather advises us to know that vengeance belongs to God.

"Honor everyone. Love the brotherhood. Fear God. Honor the emperor. Servants, be subject to your masters with all respect, not only to the good and gentle but also to the unjust" (1 Peter 2:17-18)

Christ is our example. When the Lord was being taken for crucifixion, He did not revile against those who reviled Him, He suffered and did not threaten to put His offenders to suffering. He bore our sins in His body on the Cross that we might live a righteous life after dying to sin. By His wounds we are healed of our sin. We all have gone astray like sheep but the Lord had mercy on us to reconcile to the Father. Now the Lord Jesus Christ desires that we offer up living sacrifices to God through Him.

"For to this you have been called, because Christ also suffered for you, leaving you an example, so that you might follow in his steps. He committed no sin, neither was deceit found in his

mouth. When he was reviled, he did not revile in return; when he suffered, he did not threaten, but continued entrusting himself to him who judges justly. He himself bore our sins in his body on the tree, that we might die to sin and live to righteousness. By his wounds you have been healed. 25 For you were straying like sheep, but have now returned to the Shepherd and Overseer of your souls" (1 Peter 2:21-25)

www.ingramcontent.com/pod-product-compliance
Lightning Source LLC
Chambersburg PA
CBHW071859020426
42331CB00010B/2594